The Philistines:

R.A.S. Macalister

PREFACE

AMONG the Nations that came within the purview of the Old Testament Writers—nations seldom mentioned without stricture, whether for idolatry, immorality, or cruelty—perhaps none were the object of so concentrated an aversion as were the Philistines. The licentiousness of the Amorites, the hard-heartedness of the Egyptian taskmasters, the fiendish savagery of the Assyrian warriors, each of these in turn receives its due share of condemnation. But the scornful judgement passed by the Hebrews on the Philistines has made a much deeper impression on the Bible-reading West than have their fulminations against other races and communities with which they had to do. In English, from at least the time of Dekker, 1 the word 'Philistine' has been used in one or other of the senses of the modern colloquialism 'outsider'; and, especially since the publication of the essays of Mr. Matthew Arnold, it has become almost a technical term for a person boorish or bucolic of mind, impervious to the higher influences of art or of civilization. In French and German—probably, indeed, in most of the languages of Europe—the word is used in familiar speech with a greater or less approximation to the same meaning.

The following little book is an attempt to collect in a convenient form the information so far available about the Philistine people. It is an expansion of a course of three lectures, delivered in 1911 before the British Academy under the Schweich Fund. In preparing it for publication, the matter has been revised and re-written throughout; and the division into lectures—primarily imposed by the exigencies of time-allowance—has been abandoned for a more systematic and convenient division into chapters and sections.

It is hoped that the perusal of these pages will at least suggest a doubt as to the justice of the colloquial use of the name of this ancient people.

As it may be well to preserve a record of the syllabus of the original lectures, a copy of it is subjoined.

Lecture I (15 December, 1911). The evil reputation of the Philistines. Recent researches and discoveries. A sketch of the development of Cretan civilization. The Keftiu in the Egyptian records. The sack of Cnossos and subsequent developments. The 'Peoples of the Sea'. Their raid on Egypt. Its repulse. Recovery of the 'Peoples of the Sea' from their reverse. The adventures of Wen-Amon. The earliest reference to the Philistines in the Old Testament. The Abraham and Isaac stories. The references in the history of the Exodus. Shamgar. Samson.

Lecture II (18 December, 1911). The domination of the Philistines. The capture of the Ark and the outbreak of plague. Samuel and Saul. Relative culture of Philistines and Hebrews during the reign of Saul. The incidents of David's outlawry. Achish, king of Gath. Gilboa. The Philistine domination broken by David. The various versions of the story of Goliath. The Philistines under the later monarchy. The Philistines in the Assyrian records. Nehemiah. The Maccabees. Traditions of the Philistines among the modern peasants of Palestine. Theories of the origin of the Philistines. Caphtor and the Cherethites.

Lecture III (22 December, 1911). The Organization of the Philistines. Their country and cities. The problem of the site of Ekron. The language of the Philistines. Alleged traces of it in Hebrew. Their religion and deities. Their art. Recent discoveries. The place of the Philistines in History and civilization.

I have to express my acknowledgements to my friends and colleagues, the Rev. P. Boylan, Maynooth, and the Rev. Prof. Henry Browne, S. J.; also to the Very Rev. Principal G. A. Smith, Aberdeen, and Mr. E. H. Alton, of Dublin University, for allowing me to consult them on various points that arose in the course of this work. The first and last named have most kindly read through proof-sheets of the work and have made many valuable suggestions, but they have no responsibility for any errors that the discerning critic may detect.

The figures on pp. 118, 119 are inserted by permission of the Society for Promoting Christian Knowledge.

R. A. S. M.

DUBLIN,
New Year, 1913.

Footnotes

xv:1 The *New English Dictionary* quotes, *inter alia*, 'Silke and satten, you mad Philistines, silke and satten' (Dekker, 1600): 'They say, you went to Court last Night very drunk; nay, I'm told for certain you had been among Philistines' (Swift, 1738): 'The obtuseness of a mere English Philistine we trust is pardonable' (*The Examiner*, 1827): 'Philistinism! we have not the expression in English. Perhaps we have not the word because we have so much of the thing' (M. Arnold. 1863): and the quotation from the *Quarterly Review*, which is printed on the title-page.

THE PHILISTINES THEIR HISTORY AND CIVILIZATION
CHAPTER I. THE ORIGIN OF THE PHILISTINES

THE Old Testament history is almost exclusively occupied with Semitic tribes. Babylonians, Assyrians, Canaanites, Hebrews, Aramaeans—all these, however much they might war among themselves, were bound by close linguistic and other ties, bespeaking a common origin in the dim, remote recesses of the past. Even the Egyptians show evident signs of having been at least crossed with a Semitic strain at some period early in their long and wonderful history. One people alone, among those brought conspicuously to our notice in the Hebrew Scriptures, impresses the reader as offering indications of alien origin. This is the people whom we call 'Philistines'.

If we had any clear idea of what the word 'Philistine' meant, or to what language it originally belonged, it might throw such definite light upon the beginnings of the Philistine people that further investigation would be unnecessary. The answer to this question is, however, a mere matter of guess-work. In the Old Testament the word is regularly written Pᵉlištīm (פְּלִשְׁתִּים), singular Pᵉlištī (פְּלִשְׁתִּי), twice 1 Pᵉlištīyim (פְּלִשְׁתִּיִּים), The territory which they inhabited during the time of their struggles with the Hebrews is known as 'ereṣ Pᵉlištim (אֶרֶץ פְּלִשְׁתִּים) 'the Land of Philistines', or in poetical passages, simply Pelešeth (פְּלָשֶׁת) 'Philistia'. Josephus regularly calls them Παλαιστινοί, except once, in his version of the Table of Nations in Genesis x (*Ant.* I. vi. 2) where we have the genitive singular Φυλιστίνου.

Various conjectures as to the etymology of this name have been put forward from time to time. One of the oldest, that apparently due to Fourmont, 1 connects it with the traditional Greek name Πελασγοί; an equation which, however, does no more than move the problem of origin one step further back. This theory was adopted by Hitzig, the author of the first book in modern times on the Philistines, 2 Who connected the word with Sanskrit valakṣa 'white', and made other similar comparisons, as for instance between the name of the deity of Gaza, *Marna*, and the Indian *Varuna*. On the other hand a Semitic etymology was sought by Gesenius, 3 Movers, 4 and others, who quoted an Ethiopic verb *falasa*, 'to wander, roam,' whence comes the substantive *fallási*, 'a stranger.' In this etymology they were anticipated by the translators of the Greek Version, who habitually render the name of the Philistines by the Greek word ἀλλόφυλοι, 5 even when it is put into the mouths of Goliath or Achish, when speaking of themselves. Of course this is merely an etymological speculation op the part of the translators, and proves nothing more than the existence of a Hebrew root (otherwise apparently unattested) similar in form and meaning to the Ethiopic root cited. And quite apart from any questions of linguistic probability, there is an obvious logical objection to such an etymology. In the course of the following pages we shall find the court scribes of Ramessu III, the historians of Israel, and the keepers of the records of the kings of Assyria, agreeing in applying the same name to the nation in question. These three groups of writers, belonging to as many separate nations and epochs of time, no doubt worked independently of each other—most probably in ignorance of each other's productions. This being so, it follows almost conclusively that the name 'Philistine' must have been derived from Philistine sources, and in short must have been the native designation. Now a word meaning 'stranger' or the like, while it might well be applied by foreigners to a nation deemed by them intruders, would scarcely be adopted by the nation itself, as its chosen ethnic appellation. This Ethiopic comparison it seems therefore safe to reject. The fantasy that Redslob 1 puts forward, namely, that תשלפ 'Philistia' was an anagram for הלפש, the *Shephelah* or foot-hills of Judea, is perhaps best forgotten: place-names do not as a rule come to be in this mechanical way, and in any case 'the Shephelah' and 'Philistia' were not geographically identical.

There is a peculiarity in the designation of the Philistines in Hebrew which has often been noticed, and which must have a certain significance. In referring to a tribe or nation the Hebrew writers as a rule either (*a*) personified an imaginary founder, making his name stand for the tribe supposed to derive from him—e. g. 'Israel' for the Israelites; or (*b*) used the tribal name *in the singular*, with the definite article—a usage sometimes transferred to the Authorized Version, as in such familiar phrases as 'the Canaanite was then in the land' (Gen. xii. 6); but more commonly assimilated to the English idiom which requires a plural, as in 'the iniquity of the Amorite[s] is not yet full' (Gen. xv. 16). But in referring to the Philistines, the *plural* of the ethnic name is always used, and as a rule the definite article is omitted. A good example is afforded by the name of the Philistine territory above mentioned, 'ereṣ Pᵉlištīm, literally 'the land of Philistines': contrast such an expression as 'ereṣ hak-Kᵉna'anī, literally 'the land of the Canaanite'. A few other names, such as that of the *Rephaim*, are similarly constructed: and so far as the scanty monuments of Classical Hebrew permit us to judge, it may be said generally that the same usage seems to be followed when there is question of a people not conforming to the model of Semitic (or perhaps we should rather say Aramaean) tribal organization. The Canaanites, Amorites, Jebusites, and the rest, are so closely bound together by the theory of blood-kinship which even yet prevails in the Arabian deserts, that each may logically be spoken of as an *individual* human unit. No such polity was recognized among the pre-Semitic *Rephaim*, or the intruding Philistines, so that they had to be referred to as an *aggregate* of human units. This rule, it must be admitted, does not seem to be rigidly maintained; for instance, the name of the pre-Semitic *Horites* might have been expected to follow the exceptional construction. But a hard-and-fast adhesion to so subtle a distinction, by all the writers who have contributed to the canon of the Hebrew scriptures and by all the scribes who have transmitted their works, is not to be expected. Even in the case of the Philistines the rule that the definite article should be omitted is broken in eleven places. [1]

However, this distinction, which in the case of the Philistines is carefully observed (with the exceptions cited in the footnote), indicates at the outset that the Philistines were regarded as something apart from the ordinary Semitic tribes with whom the Hebrews had to do.

The name of the Philistines, therefore, does not lead us very far in our examination of the origin of this people. Our next step must be to inquire what traditions the Hebrews preserved respecting the origin of their hereditary enemies; though such evidence on a question of historical truth must obviously even under the most favourable circumstances be unsatisfactory.

The *locus classicus* is, of course, the table of nations in Genesis x. Here we read (vv. 6, 13, 14), 'And the sons of Ham: Cush, and Mizraim, and Put, and Canaan... And Mizraim begat Ludim, and 'Anamim, and Lehabim, and Naphtuhim, and Pathrusim, and Casluhim (whence went forth the Philistines) and Caphtorim.' The list of the sons of Ham is assigned to the Priestly source; that of the sons of Mizraim (distinguished by the formula 'he begat') to the Yahvistic source. The ethnical names are almost all problematical, and the part of special interest to us has been affected, it is supposed, by a disturbance of the text.

So far as the names can be identified at all, the passage means that in the view of the writer or writers who compiled the table of nations, the Hamitic or southern group of mankind were Ethiopia, Egypt, 'Put', and Canaan. Into the disputed question of the identification of the third of these, this is not the place to enter. Passing over the children assigned to Cush or Ethiopia, we come to the list of peoples supposed by the Yahvist to be derived from Egypt. Who or what most of these peoples were is very uncertain. The *Ludim* are supposed to have been Libyans (*d* in the name being looked upon as an error for *b*); the *Lehabim* are also supposed to be Libyans; the *'Anamim* are unknown, as are also the *Casluhim;* but the *Naphtuhim* and *Pathrusim* seem to be reasonably identified with the inhabitants of Lower and Upper Egypt respectively. 2 There remain the *Caphtorim*, and the interjected note 'whence went forth the Philistines'. The latter has every appearance of having originally been a marginal gloss that has crept into the text. And in the light of other passages, presently to be cited, it would appear that the gloss referred originally not to the unknown Casluhim, but to the Caphtorim. It must, however, be said that all the versions, as well as the first chapter of Chronicles, agree in the reading of the received text, though emendation would seem obviously called for. This shows us either that the disturbance of the text is of great antiquity, or else that the received text is, after all, correct, and that the Casluhim are to be considered a branch of, or at any rate a tribe nearly related to, the Caphtorim.

The connexion of the Philistines with a place called Caphtor is definitely stated in Amos ix. 7: 'Have not I brought up Israel out of the land of Egypt, *and the Philistines from Caphtor*, and the Syrians from Kir?' It is repeated in Jeremiah xlvii. 4, where the Philistines are referred to as 'the remnant of the *'i* of Caphtor'. The word *'i* is rendered in the Revised Version 'island', with marginal rendering 'sea coast': this alternative well expresses the ambiguity in the meaning of the word, which does not permit us to assume that Caphtor, as indicated by Jeremiah, was necessarily one of the islands of the sea. Indeed, even if the word definitely meant 'island', its use here would not be altogether conclusive on this point: an isolated headland might long pass for an island among primitive navigators, and therefore such a casual mention need not limit our search for Caphtor to an actual island.

Again, in Deuteronomy ii. 23, certain people called the Caphtorim, 'which came out of Caphtor', are mentioned as having destroyed the 'Avvim that dwelt in villages as far as Gaza, and established themselves in their stead. The geographical indication shows that the Caphtorim must be identified, generally speaking, with the Philistines: the passage is valuable as a record of the name of the earlier inhabitants, who, however, were not utterly destroyed: they remained in the south of the Philistine territory (Joshua xiii. 4).

The question of the identification of Caphtor must, however, be postponed till we have noted the other ethnic indications which the Hebrew scriptures preserve. Chief of these is the application of the word C^erēthi (יְתָרְכּ) 'Cherēthites' to this people or to a branch of them.

Thus in 1 Samuel xxx. 14 the young Egyptian servant, describing the Amalekite raid, said 'we raided the south of the Cherethites and the property of Judah and the south of the Calebites and burnt Ziklag with fire'. In Ezekiel xxv. 16 the Philistines and the Cherethites with the 'remnant of the sea-coast' are closely bound together in a common denunciation, which we find practically repeated in the important passage Zephaniah ii. 5, where a woe is pronounced on the dwellers by the sea-coast, the nation of the Cherethites, and on 'Canaan, the land of the Philistines'; this latter is a noteworthy expression, probably, however, interpolated in the text. In both these last passages the Greek version renders this word Κρῆτες 'Cretans '; elsewhere it simply transliterates (Χελεθί, with many varieties of spelling). 1

In both places it would appear that the name 'Cherethites' is chosen for the sake of a paronomasia (תרכ = 'to cut off'). In the obscure expression 'children of the land of the covenant' (תירבה אדץ בני Ezek. xxx. 5) some commentators 2 see a corruption of יתרכה ינב 'Children of the Cherethites'. But see the note, p. 123 *post*.

In other places the Cherethites are alluded to as part of the bodyguard of the early Hebrew kings, and are coupled invariably with the name פְּלֵתִי Pelēthites. This is probably merely a modification of פְּלִשְׁתִי, the ordinary word for 'Philistine', the letter s being omitted in order to produce an assonance between the two names. [3] The Semites are fond of such assonances: they are not infrequent in modern Arab speech, and such a combination as Shuppīm and Ḥuppīm (1 Chron. vii. 12) shows that they are to be looked for in older Semitic writings as well. If this old explanation [4] be not accepted, we should have to put the word 'Pelethites' aside as hopelessly unintelligible. Herodotus's Philitis, or Philition, a shepherd after whom the Egyptians were alleged to call the Pyramids, [5] has often been quoted in connexion with this name, coupled with baseless speculations as to whether the Philistines could have been the Hyksos.

With regard to the syntax of these two names, it is to be noticed that as a rule they conform to the ordinary Hebrew usage, contrary perhaps to what we might have expected. But in the two prophetic passages we have quoted, the name of the Cherethites agrees in construction with that of the Philistines.

In three passages—2 Samuel xx. 23, 2 Kings xi. 4, 19—the name of the royal body-guard of 'Cherethites' appears as כָּרִי 'Carians'. If this happened only once it might be purely accidental, due to the dropping of a ת by a copyist; but being confirmed by its threefold repetition, it is a fact that must be noted carefully [1] for future reference.

Here the Hebrew records leave us, and we must seek elsewhere for further light. Thanks to the discoveries of recent years, our search need not be prolonged. For in the Egyptian records we find mention of a region whose name, *Keftiu*, has an arresting similarity to the 'Caphtor' of Hebrew writers. It is not immediately obvious whence comes the final *r* of the latter, if the comparison be sound; but waiving this question for a moment, let us see what is to be made of the Egyptian name, and, above all, what indications as to its precise situation are to be gleaned from the Egyptian monuments.

The name k-f-tïw ( ) sometimes written k-f-ty-w ( ) first meets us on Egyptian monuments of the Eighteenth Dynasty. It is apparently an Egyptian word: at least, it is capable of being rendered behind', and assuming this rendering Mr. H. R. Hall [2] aptly compares it with our colloquialism 'the Back of Beyond'. Unless this is to be put aside as a mere *Volksetymologie*, it clearly would be useless to search the maps of classical atlases for any name resembling Keftiu. It would simply indicate that the Egyptians had a sense of remoteness or uncertainty about the position of the country; and even from this we could derive no help, for as a rule they manifest a similar vagueness about other foreign places.

It is specifically under Thutmose III that 'Keftiu' first appears as the name of a place or a people. On the great stele in the Cairo Museum in which the king's mighty deeds are summarized, in the form of a Hymn to Amon, we read 'I came and caused thee to smite the west-land, and the land of Keftiu and Asi ( ) are terrified'. In the Annalistic Inscription on the walls of the Temple of Karnak the name appears in interesting connexion with *maritime* enterprise. 'The harbours of the king were supplied with all the good things which he received in Syria, namely ships of Keftiu, Byblos, and Sektu [the last-named place is not identified], cedar-ships laden with poles and masts.' 'A silver vessel of Keftiu work' was part of the tribute paid to Thutmose by a certain chieftain. [1] Keftiu itself does not send any tribute recorded in the annals; but tribute from the associated land of Asi is enumerated, in which copper is the most conspicuous item. This in itself proves nothing, for the copper might in the first instance have been brought to Asi from somewhere else, before it passed into the coffers of the all-devouring Pharaoh: but on the Tell el-Amarna tablets a copper-*producing* country, with the similar name Alašia, is prominent, and as Cyprus was the chief if not the only source of copper in the Eastern Mediterranean, the balance of probability seems to be in favour of equating Asi and Alašia alike to Cyprus. In this case Keftiu would denote some place, generally speaking, in the neighbourhood of Cyprus.

The next important sources of information are the wall-paintings in the famous tombs of Sen-mut, architect to Queen Hatshepsut; of Rekhmara, vizier of Thutmose III; and of Menkheperuseneb, son of the last-named official, [2] high priest of Amon and royal treasurer. In these wall-paintings we see processions of persons, with non-Semitic European-looking faces; attired simply in highly embroidered loincloths folded round their singularly slender waists, and in high boots or gaiters; with hair dressed in a distinctly non-Semitic manner; bearing vessels and other objects of certain definite types. The tomb of Sen-mut is much injured, but the Cretan ornaments there drawn are unmistakable. In the tomb of Rekhmara we see the official standing, with five rows of foreigners carrying their gifts, a scribe recording the inventory at the head of each row, and an inscription explaining the scene as the 'Reception by the hereditary prince Rekhmara of the tribute of the south country, with the tribute of Punt, the tribute of Retenu, the tribute of Keftiu, besides the booty of all nations brought by the fame of Thutmose III'. In the tomb of Menkheperuseneb there are again two lines of tribute-bearers, described as 'the chief of Keftiu, the chief of Kheta, the chief of Tunip, the chief of Kadesh'; and an inscription asserts that these various chiefs are praising the ruler of the Two Lands, celebrating his victories, and bringing on their backs silver, gold, lapis lazuli, malachite, and all kinds of precious stones.

Fig. 1. A. A Keftian from the Tomb of Rekhmara.
B. A Cretan from Knossos.

Some minor examples, confirming the conclusions to which these three outstanding tomb-frescoes point, will be found in W. Max Müller's important paper, *Neue Darstellungen 'mykenischer' Gesandter . . . in altägyptischen Wandgemälden* (Mitt. vorderas.-Gesell., 1904, No. 2).

Recent investigations in the island of Crete have enabled us to identify with certainty the sources of the civilization which these messengers and their gifts represent. Wall-paintings have there been found representing people with the same facial type, the same costume, the same methods of dressing the hair; and as it were the originals of the costly vases they bear have been found in such profusion as to leave no doubt that they are there on their native soil. The messengers, who are depicted in the Egyptian frescoes, are introducing into Egypt some of the *chefs-d'œuvre* of Cretan art; specifically, art of the periods known as Late Minoan I and II, [1] the time of the greatest glory of the palace of Knossos; and as they are definitely described in the accompanying hieroglyphs as messengers of Keftiu, it follows that Keftiu was at least a centre of distribution of the products of Cretan civilization, and therefore a place under the influence of Crete, if it was not actually the island of Crete itself. And the clear evidence, that excavation in Crete has revealed, of a back-wash of Egyptian influence on Cretan civilization at the time of the coming to Egypt of the Keftian envoys, turns the probability into as near a certainty as it is at present possible to attain.

The next document to be noticed is a hieratic school exercise-tablet, apparently (to judge from the forms of the script) dating from the end of the Eighteenth Dynasty. It is now preserved in the British Museum, numbered 5647. ₂ On the one side are some random scribbles, like the meaningless words and phrases with which one tries a doubtful pen:

'The goddess Ubast—they are small, numerous—of precious things, when—his majesty was seen, as he turned his face there was—for the feast day, one jar of wine [this line repeated]—Ru-unti—Ru-dadama—Smdt-ty' [three names].

On the other side is

'To make names of Keftiu:

    Ašaḫurau
    Nasuy
    Akašou
    Adinai
    Pinaruta
    Rusa
    Sen-Nofer [an Egyptian name, twice repeated]
    Akašou

"a hundred of copper, *aknu*-axes" [reading uncertain]

    Beneṣasira

[two illegible names]

    Sen-nofer
    Sumrssu [Egyptian]'

Though the reading of some of the items of this list is not quite certain, it seems clear that the heading 'irt rn n keftw, 'to make names of Keftiu', indicates that this tablet is a note of names to be used in some exercise or essay. The presence of the familiar Philistine name Achish, in the form Akašou, twice over, is suggestive, but otherwise the tablet does not help forward our present inquiry into the position of Keftiu and the origin of the Philistine people.

These various discoveries of recent years make it unnecessary to discuss at any length other theories which have been presented in ancient and modern times as to the identification of the name of Keftiu or of Caphtor. The Ptolemaic Jonathan Oldbuck who translated for his master the *Decree of Canopus* into Hieroglyphics, revived this ancient geographical name to translate Φοινίκης: a piece of irresponsible pedantry which has caused nothing but confusion. Even before the discoveries of the last fifteen or twenty years it was obvious that the Keftiu of Rekhmara's tomb were as unlike Phoenicians as they could possibly be; and their gifts were also incompatible with what was known of Phoenician civilization. Endless trouble was thus given to would-be harmonists. Another antiquary of the same kind and of the same period, who drew up the inscription to be cut on the temple at Kom Ombo, has likewise made illegitimate use of the name in question. A catalogue of the places conquered by the founder of the temple, after the manner of the records of achievements of the great kings of the Eighteenth Dynasty, was *de rigueur:* so the obsequious scribe set down, apparently at random, a list of any geographical names that happened to come into his head. Among these is kptar, the final *r* of which seems to denote a Hebrew source; perhaps he learnt the name from some brother antiquary in the neighbouring Jewish colony at Aswân.

The Greek translators of the scriptures, the Peshitta, and the Targums, in Deuteronomy ii. 23, Amos ix. 7, render the name *Cappadocia*. This seems to be merely a guess, founded on similarity of sound.

In modern times, even before the days of scientific archaeology, the equation of Caphtor to *Crete* has always been the theory most in favour. Apart from Jeremiah's description of the place as an 'island'—which as we have already mentioned is not quite conclusive—the obvious equation Cherethites = Cretans would strike any student. Calmet [1] gives a good statement of the arguments for the identification which were available before the age of excavation.

For completeness' sake we may refer here to various other theories of Philistine origin which have been put forward by modern scholars: it is, however, not necessary to give full references to all the writers who have considered the question. The favourite hypothesis among those who rejected the Caphtor-Crete identification was founded on the Greek Version and Josephus: Caphtor was by them identified with Cappadocia, and Casluhim with the Colchians. Hitzig, as stated earlier in this chapter, identified them with the Pelasgians, who came, according to his view, from Crete to North Egypt, identified with the Casluhim of the Table of Nations: their language he supposed to be cognate with Sanskrit, and by Sanskrit he interpreted many of the names of people and places. Quatremère, reviewing Hitzig's book in the *Journal des Savants* (1846, pp. 257, 411), suggested a rival theory, deriving them from West Africa, equating Casluhim with Sheluḫ, a sept of the Berbers. Stark (Gaza, p. 70) assigned them to the Phoenicians, accepting the South Semitic etymology of the name Pelištim, Caphtor being the Delta, and Casluhim a name cognate with the Kasios mountain, denoting a tribe living between Kasios and Pelusium. [1] Köhler [2] had a complicated theory to reconcile all the various lines of Biblical evidence: he took Caphtor to be the Delta; the Philistines springing from there settled in Casluhim (between Casios and Pelusium): 'going forth' from Casluhim they sailed to Crete, and then returned to Philistia. Knobel (*Die Völkertafel der Genesis*, p. 215 sqq.) proposed a double origin for the Philistine people. The main body he took to be *Semites* who came out (geographically, not racially) from the Casluhim in North Egypt; and the Caphtorim were a southern tribe of Cretan or Carian origin. Knobel gave a very careful analysis of the evidence available at his time, but he overlooked the Medinet Habu sculptures, and, on the other hand, gave too much weight to the gossip of Herodotus about Philitis and the Pyramids.

Ebers [3] made an elaborate attempt to find in the Delta a site for Caphtor; but this can hardly stand against later discoveries. They are no goods from the Land of Goshen which Rekhmara's visitors are carrying. W. Max Müller [4] equates Keftiu to Cilicia, mainly on the ground of the order in which the name occurs in geographical lists: but though this is not an argument to be lightly set aside, we are confronted with the difficulty that Cilicia could hardly have been a centre of distribution of Minoan goods in the time of Rekhmara. [5]

Schwally [1] argues thus for the Semitic origin of the Philistines: that if the Philistines were immigrants, so were the Phoenicians and Syrians (*teste* Amos): that the identity of Caphtor and Crete is an unproved assumption: the Greek translation twice renders 'Cherethites' by 'Cretans', it is true, but not elsewhere, showing uncertainty on the subject: and the reading 'Crete' in Zephaniah ii. 6 is wrong. All the personal names, and all the place-names (except possibly El-tekeh and Ziklag) are Semitic, and there is no trace of any non-Semitic deity. Stade [2] asserts the Semitic origin of the people, without giving any very definite proofs; Tiele [3] claims the Philistines as Semites on the ground of their Semitic worship. Beecher (in Hastings's *Dict. of the Bible*, s. v. Philistines) claims the name of the people as 'probably Semitic', but considers that most likely they were originally Aryan pirates who had become completely Semitized. The non-circumcision of the Philistines is a difficulty against assigning to them a Semitic origin; and the various Semitic elements in their names, religion, and language can most reasonably be explained by borrowing—presumably as a result of free intermarriage with Semites or Semitized aborigines.

On the other hand, it may be said at once that it is perhaps a little premature to call them Aryans. On the whole, the probability seems to be against the Philistine being an Aryan tongue—it certainly was not, if (as is not unlikely) it had affinities with Etruscan.

But these identifications are to a large extent the personal opinions of those who put them forward. The identification of Caphtor and Keftiu with Crete is so generally accepted, that there is a danger that some difficulties in the way should be overlooked. For first of all we are met with a question of philology: whence came the final *r* in the Hebrew word? It has been suggested that it might be a nominative suffix of the Keftian language. It would in any case be more probably a locative or prepositional suffix: for place-names are apt to get taken over into foreign languages in one or other of those cases, because they are generally referred to in contexts that require them; just as Ériu, the old Irish name of Ireland, has been taken over into English in its prepositional case, now spelt *Erin*. It might possibly be a plural: Mr. Alton has suggested to me a comparison with the Etruscan plural ending *er, ar, ur*. Letting the question of the exact case pass, however, as irrelevant, there are two points that must be indicated regarding the suggestion that *r* is a Keftian case-ending. In the first place, it assumes that Keftiu is, after all, not the Egyptian word it resembles, but the native 'Keftian' name for the place in question: it is incompatible with the 'Back of Beyond' theory of the meaning of the name. In the second place, it is difficult to understand how the Hebrews should have picked up a 'Keftian' case-ending or any such grammatical formative, rather than the Egyptians; for the Egyptians were brought into direct contact with Keftians, while the Hebrews arrived on the scene too late to enjoy that advantage. Ebers attempted to solve the difficulty by supposing the *r* to come from the Egyptian adjective *wr*, 'great', tacked on to the place-name. Max Muller (*Asien und Europa*, p. 390) and Wiedemann (*Orient. Litteraturzeitung*, xiii, col. 49) point out that there is no monumental evidence for such an expression, and that in any case 'Great Keftland' would be Keft-ʿā, not Keft-*wr*. The latter (loc. cit.) has an ingenious solution: in an astronomical text in the grave of Ramessu VI occurs a list of places ʿiwm3r (the land of the Amorites) pb (unidentified) and kftḥr ('Upper Kefti'). 'Caphtor', he suggests, may be a corruption of this latter expression. The hypothesis may be noted in passing, though perhaps it is not altogether convincing.

Behind this problem lies another, perhaps equally difficult: why did the Hebrews call the home-land of the Philistines by this name, which even in Egypt was already obsolete?

To this question the only reasonable answer that seems to present itself is to the effect that by the time of the Hebrews Crete or Keftiu had, with its gorgeous palaces, passed into tradition. Like the I Breasail or Avallon of Celtic tradition, the place which the Hebrew writers called 'Caphtor' was no longer a tangible country, but a dreamland of folklore, the legends of which had probably filtered into Palestine from Egypt itself. Whether Caphtor was or was not the same as the island of Crete was to the ancient Hebrew historian a question of secondary interest beside the all-important practical fact that the Philistines were obstinate in their occupation of the most desirable parts of the Promised Land. When the inspired herdsman of Tekoa spoke of the Philistines being led from Caphtor, he was probably just as unconscious of the requirements of the scientific historian as a modern herdsman who told me that a certain ancient monument on a Palestinian hill-slope belonged 'to the time of the Rūm'. He no doubt believed what he said: but who or what the Rūm may have been, or how many years or centuries or geological aeons ago they may have flourished, he neither knew nor cared.

All, then, that the Hebrews can tell us about their hereditary enemies is, that they came from a vague traditional place called Caphtor—a place by the sea, but of which they have nothing more to say. The tradition of Caphtor seems to be a tradition of the historical glories of Crete, so far as the Egyptians knew of them, and the name seems to be a tradition of the name which, for some reason not certainly known, the Egyptians applied to the source of the desirable treasures of the Cretan civilization.

Even down to late times the tradition linking Philistia with Crete persisted in one form or another. Tacitus heard it, though in a distorted form: in the oft-quoted passage *Hist.* v. 2 he confuses the Jews with the Philistines, and makes the former the Cretan refugees. [1] ΜΕΙΝΩ, Minos, is named on some of the coins of Gaza. This town was called by the name Minoa: and its god Marna was equated to 'Zeus the Crete-born.' [2]

But did the Philistines come from Crete? That is the question which we must now consider.

The last generation saw the labours of Schliemann at Troy and elsewhere, and was startled by the discovery of the splendid pre-Hellenic civilization of Mycenae. For us has been reserved the yet greater surprise of finding that this Mycenaean age was but the latest, indeed the degenerate phase of a vastly older and higher culture. Of this ancient civilization Crete was the centre and the apex.

The course of civilization in this island, from the end of the Neolithic period onwards, is divided by Sir Arthur Evans into three periods [3] which he has named Early, Middle, and Late 'Minoan' respectively, after the name of Minos the famous legendary Cretan king. Each of these three periods is further divided into subordinate periods, indicated by numbers; thus we have Early Minoan I, II, III, and so for the others. The general characters of these nine periods may now be briefly stated, with the approximate dates which Egyptian synchronisms enable us to assign.

Into the question of the origin of the early inhabitants of Crete we need not enter. That there was some connexion between Crete and Egypt in their stone-age beginnings seems on various grounds to be not improbable. [1] The neolithic Cretan artists were much like neolithic artists elsewhere. They never succeeded in attaining a very high position among workers in flint; Crete has so far produced nothing comparable with the best work of the Egyptians and the Scandinavians. Their pottery was decorated with incised or pricked patterns filled in with white powdered gypsum, to make a white pattern on a black ground.

The *Early Minoan I* period inherited this type of ornament and ware from its predecessors, but improved it. Coloured decoration now began to be used, the old incised ornaments being imitated with a wash of paint. The ornament was restricted to simple geometrical patterns such as zigzags. The pottery was made without the wheel. In this period short triangular daggers in copper are found. In *Early Minoan II* the designs are more free and graceful: simple curves appear, side by side with straight lines, towards the end of the period. The potter's wheel is introduced. Rude and primitive idols in marble, alabaster, and steatite are found. The copper daggers are likewise found, but the use of flint and obsidian is not yet wholly abandoned. In *Early Minoan III* there is not much advance in the art of the potter. We now, however, begin to find seals with a kind of hieroglyphic signs upon them, apparently imitated (in manner if not in matter) from Egyptian seals. These seem to give us the germ of the art of writing, as practised later in Crete. Scholars differ (between 2000 and 3000 B.C.) as to the proper date to assign to the end of the Early Minoan civilization: for our present purpose it is not important to discuss the causes of disagreement, or to attempt to decide between these conflicting theories.

The next period, *Middle Minoan I*, takes a great step forward. We now begin to find polychrome decoration in pottery, with elaborate geometrical patterns; we also discover interesting attempts to picture natural forms, such as goats, beetles, &c. Upon the ruins of this stage of development, which seems to have been checked by some catastrophe, are founded the glories of *Middle Minoan II*, the period of the great palace of Phaestos and of the first palace of Knossos. To this period also belongs the magnificent polychrome pottery called Kamáres ware. Another catastrophe took place: the first palace of Knossos was ruined, and the great second palace built in its place: and the period known as *Middle Minoan III* began. It was distinguished by an intense realism in art, speaking clearly of a rapid deterioration in taste. In this period we find the pictographic writing clearly developed, with a hieratic or cursive script derived from it, adapted for writing with pen and ink. The Middle Minoan period came to an end about 1600 B.C.

Late Minoan I shows a continuation of the taste for realism. Its pottery is distinguished from that of the preceding period by the convention that its designs as a rule are painted dark on a light background: in *Middle Minoan III* they are painted light on a dark background. Linear writing is now developed. The palace of Phaestos is rebuilt. Fine frescoes and admirable sculptured vases in steatite are found in this period, to which also belong the oldest remains at Mycenae, namely the famous gold deposits in the shaft tombs. In *Late Minoan II* the naturalistic figures become conventionalized, and a degeneration in art sets in which continues into *Late Minoan III*. The foreign imports found at Tell el-Amarna and thus of the time of Ikhnaton, are all of *Late Minoan III*; this affords a valuable hint for dating this phase of development.

Now while some of the earlier periods shade into one another, like the colours of a rainbow, so that it is difficult to tell where the one ends and the next begins, this is not the case of the latest periods, the changes in which have evidently been produced by violence. The chief manifestation is the destruction of Knossos, which took place, apparently as a result of invasion from the mainland, at the very end of the period known as Late Minoan II: that is to say about 1400 B.C. The inferior style called Late Minoan III—the style which till recent years we had been accustomed to call Mycenaean—succeeded at once and without any intermediate transition to the style of Late Minoan II immediately after this raid. It was evidently the degraded style that had developed in the mainland among the successful invaders, founded upon (or, rather, degenerated from) works of art which had spread by way of trade to the adjacent lands, in the flourishing days of Cretan civilization.

We have seen that in Egyptian tombs of about 1500 B.C. there are to be seen paintings of apparently Cretan messengers and merchants, called by the name of *Keftiu*, bearing Cretan goods: and in addition we find the actual tangible goods themselves, deposited with the Egyptian dead. In Palestine and elsewhere occasional scraps of the 'palace' styles come to light. But the early specimens of Cretan art found in these regions are all exotic, just as (to quote a parallel often cited in illustration) the specimens of Chinese or Japanese porcelain exhibited in London drawing-rooms are exotic; and they affect but little the inferior native arts of the places where they are found. It is not till we reach the beginning of Late Minoan III, after the sack of Knossos, that we find Minoan culture actually taking root in the eastern lands of the Mediterranean, such as Cyprus and the adjacent coasts of Asia Minor and Syria. We can hardly dissociate this phenomenon from the sack of Knossos. The very limitations of the area over which the 'Mycenaean' art has been found are enough to show that its distribution was not a result of peaceful trade. Thus, the Hittite domination of Central and Western Asia Minor was still strong enough to prevent foreign settlers from establishing themselves in those provinces: in consequence Mycenaean civilization is there absent. The spread of the debased Cretan culture over Southern Asia Minor, Cyprus, and North Syria, between 1400 and 1200 B.C.

must have been due to the movements of peoples, one incident in which was the sack of Knossos 1: and this is true, whether those who carried the Cretan art were refugees from Crete, or were the conquerors of Crete seeking yet further lands to spoil.

In short, the sack of Knossos and the breaking of the Cretan power was an episode—it may be, was the crucial and causative episode—in a general disturbance which the fourteenth to the twelfth centuries B.C. witnessed over the whole Eastern Mediterranean basin. The mutual relations of the different communities were as delicately poised as in modern Europe: any abnormal motion in one part of the system tended to upset the balance of the whole. Egypt was internally in a ferment, thanks to the eccentricities of the crazy dilettante Ikhnaton, and was thus unable to protect her foreign possessions; the nomads of Arabia, the Sutu and Habiru, were pressing from the South and East on the Palestinian and Syrian towns; the dispossessed Cretans were crowding to the neighbouring lands on the north; the might of the Hittites, themselves destined to fall to pieces not long afterwards, blocked progress northward: it is little wonder that disorders of various kinds resulted from the consequent congestion.

It is just in this time of confusion that we begin to hear, vaguely at first, of a number of little nationalities—people never definitely assigned to any particular place, but appearing now here, now there, fighting sometimes with, sometimes against, the Egyptians and their allies. And what gives these tribelets their surpassing interest is the greatness of the names they bear. The unsatisfying and contemptuous allusions of the Egyptian scribes record for us the 'day of small things' of people destined to revolutionize the world.

We first meet these tribes in the Tell el-Amarna letters. The king of Alašia (Cyprus) complains that his coasts are being raided by the *Lukku*, who yearly plunder one small town after another. 1 That indefatigable correspondent, Rib-Addi, in two letters, complains that one Biḫura has sent people of the Sutu to his town and slain certain *Sherdan* men—apparently Egyptian mercenaries in the town guard. 2 In a mutilated passage in another letter Rib-Addi mentions the *Sherdan* again, in connexion with an attempt on his own life. Then Abi-Milki reports 3 that 'the king of *Danuna* is dead, and his brother has become king after him, and his land is at peace'. It is almost the only word of peace in the whole dreary Tell el-Amarna record.

Next we hear of these tribes in their league with the Hittites against Ramessu II, when he set out to recover the ground lost to Egypt during the futile reign of Ikhnaton. 4 With the Hittites were allied people from

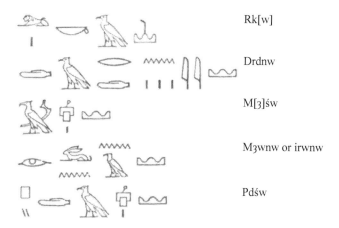

Ḳrḳš

This was in 1333 B.C. On the side of Ramessu fought mercenaries called Š3rḏ3h3 ( ) no doubt the *Sherdan* of whom we have heard already in the Tell el-Amarna letters. These people were evidently ready to sell their services to whomsoever paid for them, for we find them later operating *against* their former Egyptian masters.

About thirty years later, when Merneptah was on the throne, there was a revolt of the Libyans, and with many allies from the 'Peoples of the Sea' they proceeded to attack Egypt. Though the Philistines do not actually appear among the names of the allies, the history of this invasion is one of the most important in the *origines* of that remarkable people. The details are recorded in four inscriptions set up by the king after his victory over the invaders, one of which inscriptions is the famous 'Israel' stela.

The first inscription is that of the temple of Karnak, a translation of which will be found in Breasted's *Ancient Records*, vol. iii, p. 241. This inscription begins with a list of the allied enemies:

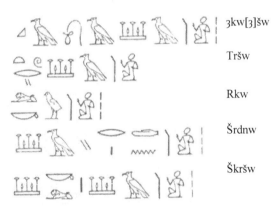

3kw[3]šw

Tršw

Rkw

Šrdnw

Škršw

The beginning of the inscription is lost, but the list is probably complete, as in the sequel, where the allied tribes are referred to more than once, no other names are mentioned.

Merneptah, after extolling his own valour and the military preparations he had made, tells us how he had received news that (Maraiwi or something similar) 'the miserable chief of Libya', with his allies aforesaid, had come with his family to the western boundary of Egypt. Enraged like a lion, he assembled his officers and to them expressed his opinion of the invaders in a way that leaves nothing to the imagination. 'They spend their time going about and fighting to fill their bellies day by day: they come to Egypt to seek the needs of their mouths: their chief is like a dog, without courage . . . .' Some of the vigorous old king's expressions have been bowdlerised by the hand of Time, which has deprived us of a course of the inscribed masonry of the temple but notwithstanding we have an admirable description of restless sea-rovers, engaged in constant plunder and piracy. Then Merneptah, strengthened by a vision of his patron Ptah which appeared to him in the night, led out his warriors, defeated the Libyans—whose 'vile fallen chief' justified Merneptah's opinion of him by fleeing, and, in the words of the official report of the Egyptian general to his master, 'he passed in safety by favour of the night . . . all the gods overthrew him for the sake of Egypt: his boasting is made void: his curses have come to roost: no one knows if he be alive or dead, and even if he lives he will never rule again. They have put in his place a brother of his who fights him whenever he sees him'. The list of slain and captives is much mutilated, but is of some importance. For the slain were reckoned by cutting off and counting the phalli of circumcised, the hands of uncircumcised victims. 1 From the classification we see that at the time of the victory of Merneptah, the Libyans were circumcised, while the Shardanu and Shekelesh and Ekwesh, as we may provisionally vocalize the names, were not circumcised. The inscription ends with the flamboyant speech of Merneptah to his court, and their reply, over which we need not linger. Nor do the other inscriptions relating to the event add anything of importance for our present purpose.

About a hundred years later we meet some of these tribes again, on the walls of the great fortified temple of Medinet Habu near Thebes, which Ramessu III, the last of the great kings of Egypt, built to celebrate the events of his reign. These events are recorded in sculptured scenes, interpreted and explained by long hieroglyphic inscriptions. It is deplorable that the latter are less informing than they might have been: we grudge bitterly the precious space wasted in grovelling compliments to the majesty of the victorious monarch, and we would have gladly dispensed with the obscure and would-be poetical style which the writer of the inscription affected. 2

Ramessu III came to the throne about 1200 B.C. 3 Another Libyan invasion menaced the land in his fifth year, but the energetic monarch, who had already been careful to organize the military resources of Egypt, was successful in beating it back. War-galleys from the northern countries, especially the *Purasati* and the *Zakkala*, accompanied the invading Libyans; but this latter element in the assault was only a foretaste of the yet more formidable attack which they were destined to make on Egypt three years later—that is to say, roughly about 1192 B.C.

The inscription describing this war is engraved on the second pylon of the temple of Medinet Habu. Omitting a dreary encomium of the Pharaoh, with which it opens, and a long hymn of triumph with which it ends, we may confine our attention to the historical events recorded in the hieroglyphs, and pictured in the representations of battles that accompany them. The inscription records how the Northerners were disturbed, and proceeded to move eastward and southward, swamping in turn the land of the Hittites, Carchemish, Arvad, Cyprus, Syria, and other places in the sane region. We are thus to picture a great southward march through Asia Minor, Syria, and Palestine. Or, rather, we are to imagine a double advance, by land and by sea: the landward march, which included two-wheeled ox-carts for the women and children, as the accompanying picture indicates; and a sea expedition, in which no doubt the spare stores would be carried more easily than on the rough Syrian roads. Clearly they were tribes accustomed to sea-faring who thus ventured on the stormy Mediterranean; clearly too, it was no mere military expedition, but a migration of wanderers accompanied by their families and seeking a new home. 1

The principal elements in the great coalition are the following:

as well as the Škrš3w, of which we have heard in previous documents.

'With hearts confident and full of plans', as the inscription says, they advanced by land and by sea to Egypt. But Ramessu was ready to 'trap them like wild-fowl'. He strengthened his Syrian frontier, and at the same time fortified the harbours or river mouths 'with warships, galleys, and barges'. The actual battles are not described, though they are pictured in the accompanying cartoons: but the successful issue of these military preparations is graphically recorded. 'Those who reached my boundary,' says the king, 'their seed is not: their heart and their soul are finished for ever and ever. As for those who had assembled before them on the sea . . . they were dragged, overturned, and laid low upon the beach: slain and made heaps from end to end of their galleys, while all their things were cast upon the water.'

The scenes in which the land and naval engagements are represented are of great importance, in that they are contemporary records of the general appearance of the invaders and of their equipment. The naval battle, the earliest of which any pictorial record remains, is graphically portrayed. We see the Egyptian archers sweeping the crews of the invading vessels almost out of existence, and then closing in and finishing the work with their swords; one of the northerners' vessels is capsized and those of its crew who swim to land are taken captive by the Egyptians waiting on the shore. In later scenes we see the prisoners paraded before the king, and the tale of the victims—counted by enumerating the hands chopped off the bodies.

The passage in the great Harris Papyrus, which also contains a record of the reign of Ramessu III, 1 adds very little to the information afforded us by the Medinet Habu inscription. The 'Danaiuna' are there spoken of as islanders. We are told that the Purasati and the Zakkala were 'made ashes', while the Shekelesh (called in the Harris Papyrus *Shardani*, who thus once more appear *against* Egypt) and the Washasha were settled in strongholds and bound. From all these people the king claims to have levied taxes in clothing and in grain.

As we have seen, the march of the coalition had been successful until their arrival in Egypt. The Hittites and North Syrians had been so crippled by them that Ramessu took the opportunity to extend the frontier of Egyptian territory northward. We need not follow this campaign, which does not directly concern us: but it has this indirect bearing on the subject, that the twofold ravaging of Syria, before and after the great victory of Ramessu, left it weakened and opened the door for the colonization of its coast-lands by the beaten remnant of the invading army.

Ramessu III died in or about 1167 B.C., and the conquered tribes began to recover their lost ground. For that powerful monarch was succeeded by a series of weak ghost-kings who disgraced the great name of Ramessu which, one and all, they bore. More and more did they become puppets in the hands of the priesthood, who cared for nothing but enriching the treasures of their temples. The frontier of Egypt was neglected. Less than a hundred years after the crushing defeat of the coalition, the situation was strangely reversed, as one of the most remarkable documents that have come down to us from antiquity allows us to see. This document is the famous Golénischeff papyrus, now at St. Petersburg. But before we proceed to an examination of its contents we must review the Egyptian materials, which we have now briefly set forth, a little more closely.

The names of the tribes, with some doubtful exceptions, are easily equated to those of peoples living in Asia Minor. We may gather a list of them out of the various authorities which have been set out above, adding to the Egyptian consonant-skeleton a provisional vocalization, and remembering that *r* and *l* are interchangeable in Egyptian:

		Tell el-Amarna *c.* 1400 B.C.	Ramessu II 1333 B.C.	Merneptah *c.* 1300 B.C.	Ramessu III *c.* 1198 B.C.
1.	Lukku	X	X	X	-
2.	Sherdanu	X	X	X	X
3.	Danunu	X	-	-	X
4.	Dardanu	-	X	-	-
5.	Masa	-	X	-	-
6.	Mawuna *or* Yaruna (?)	-	X	-	-
7.	Pidasa	-	X	-	-
8.	Kelekesh	-	X	-	-
9.	Ekwesh	-	-	X	-
10.	Turisha	-	-	X	-
11.	Shekelesh	-	-	X	X
12.	Pulasati	-	-	-	X
13.	Zakkala	-	-	-	X
14.	Washasha	-	-	-	X

An X denotes 'present in', a - 'absent from' the lists. The majority of these fourteen names too closely resemble names known from classical sources for the resemblance to be accidental. It will be found that almost every one of these names can be easily identified with the name of the coast dwellers of Asia Minor; and *vice versa*, with one significant exception, the coast-land regions of Asia Minor are all to be found in recognizable forms in the Egyptian lists. The *-sha* or *-shu* termination is to be neglected as an ethnic formative.

Thus, beginning with the Hellespont, the TROAS is represented in the *Turisha*, who have been correctly identified with the future TYRRHENIANS (Tursci) as are the *Pulasati* with the future PHILISTINES. DARDANUS in the Troad is represented by the *Dardanu*. They are the carriers of the Trojan traditions to Italy. 1 MYSIA is represented by the *Masa*, Lydia by the *Sherdanu* from the town of SARDIS. These are the future SARDINIANS. And the more inland region of MAEONIA is echoed in the *Mawuna*, if that be the correct reading. We now come to a gap: the Carians, at the S.V. corner of Asia Minor, do not appear in any recognizable form in the list, except that the North Carian town of PEDASUS seems to be echoed by the *Pidasa*. To this hiatus we shall return presently. The LYCIANS are conspicuous as the *Lukku*.

The name of the sea-coast region of Pamphylia is clearly a later appellation, expressive of the variety of tribes and nationalities which has always characterized the Levant coast. The inland Pisidian town of SAGALASSUS finds its echo in the *Shekelesh*. The CILICIANS are represented by the *Kelekesh*, and this brings us to the corner between Asia Minor and North Syria.

The only names not represented in the foregoing analysis are the *Danunu, Ekwesh*, and the three tribes which first appear in the Ramessu III invasion, the *Pulasati, Zakkala*, and *Washasha*. The first two of these, it is generally agreed, are to be equated to the DANAOI and the ACHAEANS [2]—the first appearance in historic record of these historic names. The latter do not appear in the Ramessu III lists: there were no Achaeans in the migration from Asia Minor. The *Pulasati* are unquestionably to be equated to the future PHILISTINES, north of whom we find later the *Zakkala* settled on the Palestinian coast. The *Washasha* remain obscure, both in origin and fate; but a suggestion will be made presently regarding them. They can hardly have been the ancestors of the Indo-European OSCANS.

The various lines of evidence which have been set forth in the preceding pages indicate Crete or its neighbourhood as the probable land of origin of this group of tribes. They may be recapitulated:

(1) The Philistines, or a branch of them, are sometimes called Cherethites or Cretans.

(2) They are said to come from Caphtor, a name more like Keftiu than anything else, which certainly denotes a place where the Cretan civilization was dominant.

(3) The hieratic school-tablet mentions 'Akašou' as a Keftian name: it is also Philistine [Achish].

To this may be added the important fact that the Phaestos disk, the inscription on which will be considered later in this book, shows us among its signs a head with a plumed head-dress, very similar to that shown on the Philistine captives represented at Medinet Habu.

We must not, however, forget the fact at which we paused for a moment, that thrice the Philistine guard of the Hebrew kings are spoken of as the Carians; and that the Carians are not otherwise represented in the lists of Egyptian invaders. We are probably not to confine our search for the origin of the Zakkala-Philistine-Washasha league to Crete alone: the neighbouring strip of mainland coast probably supplied its contingent to the sea-pirates. The connexion of Caria with Crete was traditional to the time of Strabo; 'the most generally received account is that the Carians, then called Leleges, were governed by Minos, and occupied the islands; then removing to the continent, they obtained possession of a large tract of sea-coast and of the interior, by driving out the former occupiers, who were for the greater part Leleges and Pelasgi.' [1] Further, he quotes Alcaeus's expression, 'shaking a Carian crest,' which is suggestive of the plumed head-dress of the Philistines. Again, speaking of the city Caunus, on the shore opposite Rhodes, he tells us that its inhabitants 'speak the same language as the Carians, came from Crete, and retained their own laws and customs' [2]—which, however, Herodotus [3] contradicts. Herodotus indeed (*loc. cit.*) gives us the same tradition as Strabo regarding the origin of the Carians: they

'had come from the islands to the continent. For being subjects of Minos, and anciently called Leleges, they occupied the islands without paying any tribute, so far as I can find by inquiring into the remotest times; but whenever Minos required them, they manned his ships; and as Minos subdued an extensive territory, and was successful in war, the Carians were by far the most famous of all nations in those times. They also introduced three inventions which the Greeks have adopted; *of fastening crests on helmets*, putting devices on shields, and putting handles on shields. . . . After a long time the Dorians and Ionians drove the Carians out of the islands and so they came to the continent. This is the account that the Cretans give of the Carians, but the Carians do not admit its correctness, considering themselves to be autochthonous inhabitants of the continent . . . and in testimony of this they show an ancient temple of Zeus Carios at Mylasa.' If then by the Pulasati we are to fill in the hiatus in the list of Asia Minor coast-dwellers, the most reasonable explanation of the name is after all the old theory that it is to be equated with *Pelasgi*. And if the worshippers of Zeus Carios settled in Palestine, they might be expected to bring their god with them and to erect a temple to him. Now we read in 1 Samuel vii, that the Philistines came up against the Israelites who were holding a religious ceremony in Mizpah; that they were beaten back by a thunderstorm, and chased in panic from Mizpah to a place called Beth-Car (v. 11). We may suppose that the chase stopped at Beth-Car because it was within Philistine territory; but unfortunately all the efforts to identify this place, not otherwise known, have proved futile. Very likely it was not an inhabited town or village at all, but a sanctuary: it was raised on a conspicuous height (for the chase stopped *under* Beth-Car): and the name means House of Car, [1] as Beth-Dagon means House or Temple of Dagon. This obscure incident, therefore, affords one more link to the chain.

If the Cretans and the Carians together were represented by Zakkala-Pulasati-Washasha league, we might expect to find some elements from the two important islands of Rhodes and Carpathos, which lie like the piers of a bridge between Crete and the Carian mainland. And I think we may, without comparisons too far-fetched, actually find such elements. Strabo tells us [2] that a former name of Rhodes was *Ophiussa:* and we can hardly avoid at least seeing the similarity between this name and that of the Washasha. [3] And as for *Carpathos*, which Homer calls Crapathos, is it too bold to hear in this classical name an echo of the pre-Hellenic word, whatever it may have been, which the Egyptians corrupted to Keftiu, and the Hebrews to Caphtor? [4]

What then are we to make of the name of the *Zakkala* or *Zakkara?* This has hitherto proved a crux. Petrie identifies it with Zakro in Crete [5]; but as has several times been pointed out regarding this identification, we do not know how old the name Zakro may be. As we have seen that all the other tribes take their name from the coasts of Asia Minor, it is probable that the Zakkala are the Cretan contingents to the coalition: and it may be that in their name we are to see the interpretation of the mysterious *Casluhim* of the Table of Nations [1] (כסלחים being a mistake for כלסי.) The most frequently suggested identification, with the TEUCRIANS (assigned by Strabo on the authority of Callinus to a Cretan origin), is perhaps the most satisfactory as yet put forward; notwithstanding the just criticism of W. Max Müller [2] that the double *k* and the vowel of the first syllable are difficulties not to be lightly evaded. Clerinont-Ganneau [3] would equate them to a Nabatean Arab tribe, the Δαχαρηνοί, mentioned by Stephanus of Byzantium; but, as Weill [4] points out, it is highly improbable that one of the allied tribes should have been Semitic in origin; if the similarity of names be more than an accident, it is more likely that the Arabs should have borrowed it.

The conclusion indicated therefore is that the Philistines were a people composed of several septs, derived from Crete and the southwest corner of Asia Minor. Their civilization, probably, was derived from Crete, and though there was a large Carian element in their composition, they may fairly be said to have been the people who imported with them to Palestine the memories and traditions of the great days of Minos.

Footnotes

1:1 In Amos ix. 7 and in the Kethībh of 1 Chron. xiv. 10. The almost uniform rendering of the Greek version (Φυλιστιείμ) seems rather to favour this orthography. The spelling of the first syllable, Φυ, shows, however, that the modern punctuation with the *shva* is of later growth, and that in the time of the Greek translation the pronunciation still approximated rather to the form of the name as it appears in Egyptian monuments (Purasati).

2:1 *Réflexions critiques sur l'origine, l'histoire et la succession des anciens peuples* (1747), ii. 254.

2:2 F. Hitzig, *Urgeschichte and Mythologie der Philister*, Leipzig, 1845.

2:3 Gesenius, *Thesaurus, s.v.*

2:4 Movers, *Untersuchungen über die Religion and die Gottheiten der Phönizier* (1841), vol. i, p. 9.

2:5 Except (*a*) in the Hexateuch, where it is always transliterated Φυλιστιείμ, sometimes Φυλιστιίμ or Φιλιστιείμ; (*b*) in Judges x. 6, 7, 11, xiii. 1, 5, xiv. 2, where again we find the word transliterated: in some important MSS. however, including Codex Alexandrinus, ἀλλόφυλοι, is used in these passages; (*c*) in Isa. ix. 11 (English ix. 12, where we find the curious rendering Ἕλληνας, possibly indicating a variant reading in the text that lay before the translators.

3:1 *Die alttest. Namen der Bevölkerung*, p. 4; adopted by Arnold in *Ersch and Gruber's Encyclopaedia, s. v. Philister*.

4:1 Namely Joshua xiii. 2; 1 Sam. iv. 7, vii. 12, xiii. 20, xvii. 51, 52; 2 Sam. v. 19, xxi. 12, 17; 1 Chron. xi. 13; 2 Chron. xxi. 16.

4:2 For fuller particulars see Skinner's *Commentary on Genesis* (pp. 200–214). Sayce finds *Caphtor and Kasluhet* on an inscription at Kom Ombo: see Hastings's *Dictionary, s. v.* Caphtor; and Man, 1903, No. 77. But see also Hall's criticisms, ib. No. 92.

6:1 Such are Χαρρι, Χαρεθθι, Χελθι, Χελθει, Χελβει, Χελβες, Χελεμα, Χελεθθι, Χελλεθι, Χελεθιι, Χελεθοι, Χελοθθι, Χολθει, Χολλεθι, Χορεθι, Χορεθθει, Χορρι, Χορρει, Χερεθει, Χερηθει, Χερετ, Χερεθθει, Χερεθιν, Χερεοι, Χωρι, Χερηθη, Χερηθει, Χετθει, Χεττει, Οχελεθθι, Οχερεπι, Οχελβι, Χκελμι, Οχελεθ, Ρεθθι. The Pelethites appear under equally strange guises: Φελετι, Φελτι, Φελτει, Φελετιι, Φελεττει, Φελεθθι, Φελεθθιι, Φελεθθει, Φελετθει, Φελελεθθι, Ουπετ, Οχετ, Οφελτι, Οφελθι, Οφελεθθιι, Οφελετθει, Ωφελεθθει, Οπελθι, Οπελεθιν, Οπερετ, Πελεβι, Οθεθιι, Χετταιοις.

6:2 Cornill, *Das Buch des Proph. Ezek.* p. 368, followed by Toy, *Ezekiel* (in Sacred Books of O. T.), p. 88.

6:3 Possibly the instinct for triliteralism may also have been instrumental in the evolution of this form.

6:4 It is given in Lakemacher, *Observationes Philologicae* (1729), ii. 38, and revived by Ewald in his *Kritische Grammatik der hehrläischen Sprache* (1827), p. 297.

6:5 Hdt. ii. 128.

7:1 The Greek version has Χερεθί in the first of these passages, in the others Χορρι with a number of varieties of spelling, Χορρει, Χοριν, &c., all of them showing *o* as the first vowel.

7:2 *Journal of the British School at Athens*, viii (1901-2), p. 157.

8:1 The name of this chieftain's land is mutilated (*tyn'y*). Mr. Hall (*op. cit.* p. 167, *Oldest Civilisation of Greece*, p. 163) restores *Yantanay*, and renders 'Cyprus'. W. Max Müller compares with this name the word *Adinai*, found in the List of Keftian names given on p. 10.

8:2 For these tombs see Hall, *British School at Athens*, vol. x (1903–4), p. 154, and *Proc. Soc. Bib. Arch.* xxxi, Plate XVI [Sen-mut]; Wilkinson, *Manners and Customs of the Ancient Egyptians*, i, Plate II, AB. [Rekhmara]; Virey, *Mémoires de la mission en Caire*, v, p. 7 [Rekhmara], p. 197 ff [Menkheperuseneb]. In the last-named, Keftiu is translated and indexed 'Phénicie'.

10:1 See the brief summary of the various stages of Cretan culture during the Bronze Age, later in the present chapter.

10:2 See Spiegelberg, *Zeitschrift fur Assyriologie* (1893), viii. 385 (where the text is published incompletely), and W. Max Müller in *Mittheilungen der vorderasiatischen Gesellschaft*, vol. v, p. 6, where facsimiles will be found.

11:1 *Dissertations qui peuvent servir de prolegomenes de l'écriture sainte* (1720), II. ii, p. 441.

12:1 A place which, as has often been noticed, has the same radicals as the name of the Philistines.

12:2 *Lehrbuch d. bibl. Geschichte*, vol. i.

12:3 *Aegypten and des Buch Mose*, p. 127 ff.

12:4 *Asien and Europa*, p. 337.

12:5 An elaborate refutation of the Cilician hypothesis will be found in Noordtzij, *De Filistijnen*, p. 31.

13:1 *Zeitschr. für wissensch. Theologie*, xxxiv (1891), p. 103.

13:2 *Gesch. des Volk. Isr.* i. 142.

13:3 *Geschiedenis van den Godsdienst in de Oudheid*, i. pp. 214, 241.

15:1 'Iudaeos Creta Insula profugos nouissima Libyae insedisse memorant, qua tempestate Saturnus ui Iouis pulsus cesserit regnis.'

15:2 Stephanus of Byzantium, s. v. ....

15:3 The bare outline statement, which is all that is necessary here, can be supplemented by reference to any of the numerous books that have appeared recently on the special subject of Cretan excavation: such as Professor Burrows's pleasantly. written work entitled *The Discoveries in Crete* (London, Murray, 1907), which contains a most useful bibliography.

16:1 See Hall, *Proc. Soc. Biblical Archaeology*, xxxi, pp. 144–148.

18:1 Other causes were at work producing the same result of restlessness among the peoples. Thus Mr. Alton suggests to me that the collapse of the island of Thera must have produced a considerable disturbance of population in the neighbouring lands.

19:1 *T.A. Letters*, ed. Winckler, No. 28; ed. Knudtzon, No. 38.

19:2 ib. W. 77, K. 123. See also W. 100.

19:3 ib. W. 151, K. 151.

19:4 For an exhaustive study of the great battle of Kadesh between Ramessu and the united tribes, see Breasted, The Battle of Kadesh (Univ. of Chicago Decennial Publications, Ser. I, No. 5.

21:1 See W. Max Müller's important note in *Proc. Soc. Bib. Arch.* x, pp. 147–154, where reasons are given against the exactly opposite interpretation, followed by 1 many authorities (e. g. Breasted, *Ancient Records*). On the other hand the contrary practice seems to be indicated by 1 Sam. xviii. 25. The difficulty of rendering lies in the fact that we have to deal with Egyptian words not found elsewhere.

21:2 See Breasted, *Ancient Records*, iv, pp. 1–85.

21:3 Petrie says 1202, Breasted 1198.

22:1 The details of these sculptures are more fully described later in this book.

23:1 Breasted, *op. cit.* p. 201.

25:1 Turisha has also been identified with the Cilician town of Tarsus.

25:2 With reservations: see Weill, *Revue archéologique, sér.* IV, vol. iii, p. 67. And even the identification of the Danaoi is uncertain. It is at least improbable that Rib-Addi of Tyre, in the letter quoted above, should report on the peacefulness of so remote a people as the Danaoi.

26:1 Strabo, XIV. ii. 17.

26:2 Strabo, xiv. ii. 3.

26:3 i. 17–1.

27:1 Βαιθχόρin the Greek Version (in some MSS. -κορ). Cf. the first footnote on p. 7.

27:2 xiv. ii. 7.

27:3 Hall looks for the Washasha in Crete, and finds them in the name of the Cretan town Fάξος [*Oldest Civilization of Greece*, p. 177]. But if this comparatively obscure Cretan name were really represented in the Egyptian lists, we might reasonably look for the more important names to appear also. The name appears (in the form *Oašašios*) in an inscription from Halicarnassus: see Weill in *Revue archéologique*, sér. IV, vol. iii, p. 63.

27:4 Baur, *Amos*, p. 79, has already suggested this identification.

27:5 *Proc. Soc. Bib. Arch.*, 1941, p. 41.

28:1 Gen. x. 14.

28:2 *Mittheil. der corderas. Gesellschaft*, v, p. 3. On *Teucer* see Frazer, *Adonis, Allis, Osiris*, p. 112.

28:3 *Recueil d'Archéologie orientale*, iv. 230.

28:4 *loc. cit.* p. 64.

CHAPTER II. THE HISTORY OF THE PHILISTINES

I. The Adventures of Wen-Amon among them

THE Golénischeff papyrus 1 was found in 1891 at El-Khibeh in Upper Egypt. It is the personal report of the adventures of an Egyptian messenger to Lebanon, sent on an important semi-religious, semi-diplomatic mission. The *naïveté* of the style makes it one of the most vivid and convincing narratives that the ancient East affords.

Ramessu III is nominally on the throne, and the papyrus is dated in his fifth year. The real authority at Thebes is, however, Hrihor, the high priest of Amon, who is ultimately to usurp the sovereignty and become the founder of the Twenty-first Dynasty. In Lower Egypt, the Tanite noble Nesubenebded, in Greek Smendes, has control of the Delta. Egypt is in truth a house divided against itself.

On the sixteenth day of the eleventh month of the fifth year of Ramessu, one Wen-Amon was dispatched from Thebes to fetch timber for the barge called *User-het*, the great august sacred barge of Amon-Ra, king of the gods. Who Wen-Amon may have been, we do not certainly know; he states that he had a religious office, but it is not clear what this was. It speaks eloquently for the rotten state of Egypt at the time, however, that no better messenger could be found than this obviously incompetent person—a sort of Egyptian prototype of the Rev. Robert Spalding! With him was an image of Amon, which he looked upon as a kind of fetish, letters of credit or of introduction, and the wherewithal to purchase the timber.

Sailing down the Nile, Wen-Amon in due time reached Tanis, and presented himself at the court of Nesubenebded, who with his wife Tentamon, received the messenger of Amon-Ra with fitting courtesy. He handed over his letters, which (being themselves unable to decipher them) they caused to be read: and they said, 'Yea, yea, I will do all that our lord Amon-Ra saith.' Wen-Amon tarried at Tanis till a fortnight had elapsed from his first setting out from Thebes; and then his hosts put him in charge of a certain Mengebti, captain of a ship about to sail to Syria. This was rather casual; evidently Mengebti's vessel was an ordinary trading ship, whereas we might have expected (and as appears later the Syrians did expect) that one charged with an important special message should be sent in a special ship. At this point the thoughtless Wen-Amon made his first blunder. He forgot all about reclaiming his letters of introduction from Nesubenebded, and so laid up for himself the troubles even now in store for the helpless tourist who tries to land at Beirut without a passport. Like the delightful pilgrimage of the mediaeval Dominican Felix Fabri, the *modernness* of this narrative of antiquity is not one of its least attractions.

On the first day of the twelfth month Mengebti's ship set sail. After a journey of unrecorded length the ship put in at Dor, probably the modern Tantura on the southern coast of the promontory of Carmel. Dor was inhabited by Zakkala (a very important piece of information) and they had a king named Badyra. We are amazed to read that, apparently as soon as the ship entered the harbour, this hospitable monarch sent to Wen-Amon 'much bread, a jar of wine, and a joint of beef'. I verily believe that this was a tale got up by some bakhshish-hunting huckster. The simpleminded tourist of modern days is imposed upon by similar magnificent fables.

There are few who have travelled much by Levant steamers without having lost something by theft. Sufferers may claim Wen-Amon as a companion in misfortune. As soon as the vessel touched at Dor, some vessels of gold, four vessels and a purse of silver—in all 5 *deben* or about 1 1/5 lb. of gold and 31 *deben* or about 7½ lb. of silver—were stolen by a man of the ship, who decamped. This was all the more serious, because, as appears later, these valuables were actually the money with which Wen-Amon had been entrusted for the purchase of the timber.

So Wen-Amon did exactly what he would have done in the twentieth century AḌ. He went the following morning and interviewed the governor, Badyra. There was no Egyptian consul at the time, so he was obliged to conduct the interview in person. 'I have been robbed in thy harbour,' he says, 'and thou, being king, art he who should judge, and search for my money. The money indeed belongs to Amon-Ra, and Nesubenebded, and Hrihor my lord: it also belongs to Warati, and Makamaru, and Zakar-Baal prince of Byblos' —the last three being evidently the names of the merchants who had been intended to receive the money. The account of Abraham's negotiations with the Hittites is not more modern than the king's reply. We can feel absolutely certain that he said exactly the words which Wen-Amon puts in his mouth: 'Thy honour and excellency! Behold, I know nothing of this complaint of thine. If the thief were of my land, and boarded the ship to steal thy treasure, I would even repay it from mine own treasury till they found who the thief was. But the thief belongs to thy ship (so I have no responsibility). Howbeit, wait a few days and I will seek for him.' Wen-Amon had to be content with this assurance. Probably nothing was done after he had been bowed out from the governor's presence: in any case, nine days elapsed without news of the missing property. At the end of the time Wen-Amon gave up hope, and made up his mind to do the best he could without the money. He still had his image of Amon-Ra, and he had a child-like belief that the foreigners would share the reverent awe with which he himself regarded it. So he sought permission of the king of Dor to depart.

Here comes a lacuna much to be deplored. A sadly broken fragment helps to fill it up, but consecutive sense is unattainable. 'He said unto me "Silence!" . . . and they went away and sought their thieves . . . and I went away from Tyre as dawn was breaking . . . Zakar-Baal, prince of Byblos. . . there I found 30 *deben* of silver and took it . . . your silver is deposited with me . . . I will take it . . . they went away . . . I came to . . . the harbour of Byblos and . . . to Amon, and I put his goods in it. The prince of Byblos sent a messenger to me . . . my harbour. I sent him a message . . .' These, with a few other stray words, are all that can be made out. It seems as though Wen-Amon tried to recoup himself for his loss by appropriating the silver of some one else. At any rate, the fragment leaves Wen-Amon at his destination, the harbour of Byblos. Then the continuous text begins again. Apparently Zakar-Baal has sent a message to him to begone and to find a ship going to Egypt in which he could sail. Why Zakar-Baal was so inhospitable does not appear. Indeed daily, for nineteen days, he kept sending a similar message to the Egyptian, who seems to have done nothing one way or another. At last Wen-Amon found a ship about to sail for Egypt, and made arrangements to go as a passenger in her, despairing of ever carrying out his mission. He put his luggage on board and then waited for the darkness of night to come on board with his image of Amon, being for some reason anxious that none but himself should see this talisman.

But now a strange thing happened. One of the young men of Zakar-Baal's entourage was seized with a prophetic ecstasy—the first occurrence of this phenomenon on record—and in his frenzy cried, Bring up the god! Bring up Amon's messenger that has him! Send him, and let him go.' Obedient to the prophetic message Zakar-Baal sent down to the harbour to summon the Egyptian. The latter was much annoyed, and protested, not unreasonably, at this sudden change of attitude. Indeed he suspected a ruse to let the ship go off, with his belongings, and leave him defenceless at the mercy of the Byblites. The only effect of his protest was an additional order to 'hold up' the ship as well.

In the morning he presented himself to Zakar-Baal. After the sacrifice had been made in the castle by the sea-shore where the prince dwelt, Wen-Amon was brought into his presence. He was 'sitting in his upper chamber, leaning his back against a window, while the waves of the great Syrian sea beat on the shore behind him'. To adapt a passage in one of Mr. Rudyard Kipling's best-known stories, we can imagine the scene, but we cannot imagine Wen-Amon imagining it: the *eye-witness* speaks in every word of the picturesque description.

The interview was not pleasant for the Egyptian. It made so deep an impression upon him, that to our great gain he was able when writing his report to reproduce it almost verbatim, as follows:

'Amon's favour upon thee,' said Wen-Amon.

'How long is it since thou hast left the land of Amon?' demanded Zakar-Baal, apparently without returning his visitor's salutation. 'Five months and one day,' said Wen-Amon.

(This answer shows how much of the document we have lost. We cannot account for more than the fourteen days spent between Thebes and Tanis, nine days at Dor, nineteen days at Byblos—six weeks in all-plus the time spent in the voyage, which at the very outside could scarcely have been more than another six weeks.)

'Well then, if thou art a true man, where are thy credentials?'

We remember that Wen-Amon had left them with the prince of Tanis, and he said so. Then was Zakar-Baal very wroth. 'What! There is no writing in thy hand? And where is the ship that Nesubenebded gave thee? Where are its crew of Syrians? For sure, he would never have put thee in charge of this (incompetent Egyptian) who would have drowned thee—and then where would they have sought their god and thee?'

This is the obvious sense, though injured by a slight lacuna. Nothing more clearly shows how the reputation of Egypt had sunk in the interval since the exploits of Ramessu III. Zakar-Baal speaks of Mengebti and his Egyptian crew with much the same contempt as Capt. Davis in Stevenson's *Ebb-tide* speaks of a crew of Kanakas. Wen-Amon ventured on a mild protest. 'Nesubenebded has *no* Syrian crews: *all* his ships are manned with Egyptians.'

'There are twenty ships in my harbour,' said Zakar-Baal sharply, and ten thousand ships in Sidon—' The exaggeration and the aposiopesis vividly mirror the vehemence of the speaker. He was evidently going on to say that these ships, though Egyptian, were all manned by Syrians. But, seeing that Wen-Amon was, as he expresses it, 'silent in that supreme moment' he broke off, and abruptly asked—

'Now, what is thy business here?'

We are to remember that Wen-Amon had come to buy timber, but had lost his money. We cannot say anything about whether he had actually recovered the money or its equivalent, because of the unfortunate gap in the document already noticed. However, it would appear that he had at the moment no ready cash, for he tried the effect of a little bluff. 'I have come for the timber of the great august barge of Amon-Ra, king of the gods. Thy father gave it, as did thy grandfather, and thou wilt do so too.'

But Zakar-Baal was not impressed. 'True,' said he, 'they gave the timber, but they were paid for it: I will do so too, if I be paid likewise.' And then we are interested to learn that he had his father's account-books brought in, and showed his visitor the records of large sums that had been paid for timber. 'See now,' continued Zakar-Baal in a speech rather difficult to construe intelligibly, 'had I and my property been under the king of Egypt, he would not have sent money, but would have sent a command. These transactions of my father's were not the payment of tribute due. I am not thy servant nor the servant of him that sent thee. All I have to do is to speak, and the logs of Lebanon lie cut on the shore of the sea. But where are the sails and the cordage thou hast brought to transport the logs? . . . Egypt is the mother of all equipments and all civilization; how then have they made thee come in this hole-and-corner way?' He is evidently still dissatisfied with this *soi-disant* envoy, coming in a common passenger ship without passport or credentials.

Then Wen-Amon played his trump card. He produced the image of Amon. 'No hole-and-corner journey is this, O guilty one!' said he. 'Amon owns every ship on the sea, and owns Lebanon which thou hast claimed as thine own. Amon has sent me, and Hrihor my lord has made me come, bearing this great god. And yet, though thou didst well know that he was here, thou hadst kept him waiting twenty-nine days in the harbour. 1 Former kings have sent money to thy fathers, but not life and health: if thou do the bidding of Amon, he will send thee life and health. Wish not for thyself a thing belonging to Amon-Ra.'

These histrionics, however, did not impress Zakar-Baal any more than the previous speech. Clearly Wen-Amon saw in his face that the lord of Byblos was not overawed by the image of his god, and that he wanted something more tangible than vague promises of life and health. So at length he asked for his scribe to be brought him that he might write a letter to Tanis, praying for a consignment of goods on account. The letter was written, the messenger dispatched, and in about seven weeks returned with a miscellaneous cargo of gold, silver, linen, 500 rolls of papyrus (this is important), hides, rope, lentils, and fish. A little present for Wen-Amon himself was sent as well by the lady Tentamon. Then the business-like prince rejoiced, we are told, and gave the word for the felling of the trees. And at last, some eight months after Wen-Amon's departure from Thebes, the timber lay on the shore ready for delivery.

A curious passage here follows in the papyrus. It contains one of the oldest recorded jokes—if not actually the oldest—in the world. When Zakar-Baal came down to the shore to give the timber over to Wen-Amon, he was accompanied by an Egyptian butler, by name Pen-Amon. The shadow of Zakar-Baal's parasol happened to fall on the envoy, whereupon the butler exclaimed, 'Lo, the shadow of Pharaoh thy lord falleth on thee!' The point of the witticism is obscure, but evidently even Zakar-Baal found it rather too extreme, for he sharply rebuked the jester. But he proceeded himself to display a delicate humour. 'Now,' said he, 'I have done for thee what my fathers did, though thou hast not done for me what thy fathers did. Here is the timber lying ready and complete. Do what thou wilt with it. But do not be contemplating the terror of the sea' (there cannot be the slightest doubt that Wen-Amon was at this moment glancing over the waters and estimating his chances of a smooth crossing). 'Contemplate for a moment the terror of Me! Ramessu IX sent some messengers to me and'—here he turned to the butler—' Go thou, and show him their *graves*!'

'Oh, let me not see them!' was the agonized exclamation of Wen-Amon, anxious now above all things to be off without further delay. Those were people who had no *god* with them! Wherefore dost thou not instead erect a tablet to record to all time "that Amon-Ra sent to me and I sent timber to Egypt, to beseech ten thousand years of life, and so it came to pass"?'

'Truly that would be a great testimony!' said the sarcastic prince, and departed.

Wen-Amon now set about loading his timber. But presently there sailed eleven ships of the Zakkala into the harbour—possibly those on whom he had made a rash attempt at piracy to recoup himself for his losses at Dor. The merchants in them demanded his arrest. The poor Egyptian sat down on the shore and wept. 'They have come to take me *again*!' he cried out—it would appear that he had been detained by the Zakkala before, but the record of this part of his troubles is lost in one of the lacunae of the MS. We despair of him altogether when he actually goes on to tell us that when news of this new trouble reached Zakar-Baal, that magnate wept also. However, we need not question the charming detail that he sent to Wen-Amon an Egyptian singing-girl, to console him with her songs. But otherwise he washed his hands of the whole affair. He told the Zakkala that he felt a delicacy about arresting the messenger of Amon on his own land, but he gave them permission to follow and arrest him themselves, if they should see fit. So away Wen-Amon sailed, apparently without his timber, and presumably with the Zakkala in pursuit. But he managed to evade them. A wind drove him to Cyprus. The Cypriotes came out, as he supposed, to kill him and his crew; but they brought them before Hatiba, their queen. He called out 'Does any one here understand Egyptian?' One man stepped forward. He dictated a petition to be translated to the queen—

And here the curtain falls abruptly, for the papyrus breaks off; and the rest of this curious tragi-comedy of three thousand years ago is lost to us.

We see from it that the dwellers on the Syrian coast had completely thrown off the terror inspired by the victories of Ramessu III. An Egyptian on a sacred errand from the greatest men in the country, bearing the image of an Egyptian god, could be robbed, bullied, mocked, threatened, thwarted in every possible way. Granted that he was evidently not the kind of man to command respect, yet the total lack of reverence for the royalties who had sent him, and the sneers at Egypt and the Egyptian rulers, are very remarkable.

We see also that the domain of the 'People of the Sea' was more extensive than the scanty strip of territory usually allowed them on Bible maps. Further evidence of this will meet us presently, but meanwhile it may be noted that the name 'Palestine' is much less of an *extension* of the name 'Philistia' than the current maps would have us suppose. In other words, the two expressions are more nearly synonymous than they are generally taken to be. We find Dor, south of Carmel, to be a Zakkala town; and Zakkala ships are busy in the ports further north.

Indeed, one is half inclined to see Zakkala dominant at Byblos itself. Wen-Amon was a person of slender education—even of his own language he was not a master—and he was not likely to render foreign names correctly. Probably he could speak nothing but Egyptian: he was certainly ignorant of the language of Cyprus, whatever that may have been: and possibly linguistic troubles are indicated by his rendering of the name of the lord of Byblos. Can it be that this was not a name at all, but a title (or rather the Semitic translation of a title, given by a Zakkala dragoman): that Zakar is not רכז 'remember', but the name of the *Zakkala:* and that Baal here, as frequently elsewhere, means 'lord' in a human and not a divine sense? If so, the name would mean 'the lord of the Zakkala', a phrase that recalls 'the lords of the Philistines' in the Hebrew Scriptures. The syntax assumed is of course quite un-Semitic: but it is often the case in dragomans' translations that the syntax of the original language is preserved. Something like this idea has been anticipated by M. A. J. Reinach. [1]

Zakar-baal was no mere pirate chieftain, however. He was a substantial, civilized, and self-reliant prince, and contrasts most favourably with the weak, half-blustering, half-lacrimose Egyptian. He understood the Egyptian language; for he could rebuke the jest of his Egyptian butler, who would presumably speak his native tongue in 'chaffing' his compatriot; and no doubt the interview in the upper room was carried on in Egyptian. He was well acquainted with the use of letters, for he knew where to put his finger on the relevant parts of the accounts of his two predecessors. These accounts were probably *not* in cuneiform characters on clay tablets, as he is seen to import large quantities of papyrus from Egypt. He is true to his old maritime traditions: he builds his house where he can watch the great waves of the Mediterranean beat on the shore, and he is well informed about the ships in his own and the neighbouring harbours, and their crews.

There is a dim recollection of a Philistine occupation of Phoenicia recorded for us in an oft-quoted passage of Justin (xviii. 3. 5), 1 in which he mentions a raid by the king of Ashkelon, just before the fall of Troy, on the Phoenician town of Sidon (so called from an alleged Phoenician word 'Sidon', meaning 'fish'). 'This is of course merely a saga-like tradition, and as we do not know from what authority Justin drew his information we can hardly put a very heavy strain upon it. And yet it seems to hang together with the other evidence, that in the Mycenaean period, when Troy was taken, there actually was a Philistine settlement on the Phoenician coast. As to the specific mention of Ashkelon, a suggestion, perhaps a little venturesome, may be hazarded. The original writer of the history of this vaguely-chronicled event, whoever he may have been, possibly recorded correctly that it was the Zakkala who raided Sidon. Some later author or copyist was puzzled by this forgotten name, and 'emended' *a rege Sacaloniorum* to *a rege Ascaloniorum*. Stranger things have happened in the course of manuscript transmission. 2

The Papyrus gives us some chronological indications of importance. The expedition of Wen-Amon took place in the fifth year of Ramessu XII, that is to say, about 1110 B.C. Zakar-Baal had already been governor of Byblos for a considerable time, for he had received envoys from Ramessu IX (1144–1129). Suppose these envoys to have come about 1130, that gives him already twenty years. The envoys of Ramessu IX were detained seventeen years; but in the first place this may have been an exaggeration, and in the second place we need not suppose that many of those seventeen years necessarily fell within the reign of the sender of these messengers. Further, Zakar-Baal's father and grandfather had preceded him in office. We do not know how long they reigned, but giving twenty-five years to each, which is probably a high estimate, we reach the date 1180, which is sufficiently long after the victory of Ramessu III for the people to begin to recover from the blow which that event inflicted on them.

Footnotes

29:1 See Max Müller, *Mittheilungen der deutschen vorderasiatischen Gesellschaft*, 1900, p. 14; Erman, *Zeitschrift far ägyptische Sprache*, xxxviii, p. 1; Breasted, *Ancient Records*, iv, p. 274.

34:1 An inconsistency: he has added ten days to his former statement.

36:1 'Byblos, où règne un prince qui pourrait bien être un Tchakara sémitisé, si l'on en croit son nom de Tchakar-baal.' *Revue archéologique*, sér. IV, vol. xv, p. 45.

37:1 'Et quoniam ad Carthaginiensium mentionem uentum est, de origine eorum pauca dicenda sunt, repetitis Tyriorum paulo altius rebus, quorum casus etiam dolendi fuerunt. Tyriorum gens condita a Phoenicibus fuit, qui terraemotu uexati, relicto patriae solo, Assyrium stagnum primo, mox mari proximum littus incoluerunt, condita ibi urbe quam a piscium ubertate Sidona appellauerunt; nam piscem Phoenices *sidon* uocant. Post multos deinde annos a rege Ascaloniorum expugnati, nauibus appulsi, Tyron urbem ante annum Troianae cladis condiderunt.'

37:2 On the other hand Scylax in his *Periplus* calls Ashkelon 'a city of the Tyrians'.

2. THEIR STRUGGLE WITH THE HEBREWS

We now turn to the various historical references to the Philistines in the Hebrew Scriptures.

It happens that the Zakkala, with whom the Golénischeff Papyrus is concerned, are not mentioned by name in the received text of the Old Testament. The southern Philistines were more conspicuous in the history of the Hebrews, and this name is in consequence used indifferently for all the tribal subdivisions of the hated enemy. The first appearance of the Philistines on the coast of Southern Palestine is not recorded in the Old Testament, but it may possibly be inferred indirectly. In the oldest monument of Hebrew speech, the Song of Deborah, the tribe of Dan is referred to as a maritime people who 'remained in ships' while their brethren bore the brunt of the invasion of Sisera. Towards the end of the Book of Judges, we find that certain of the tribe of Dan are compelled to seek a home elsewhere, and choose the fertile, well-watered, but hot and fever-haunted Laish, a place remote from everywhere, and where the people were 'quiet'—as they well might be in that malaria-stricken furnace. Why did the Danites leave for this unsatisfactory territory their healthy and rich land by the sea-coast? Probably because they were driven by pressure from without. The migration of the Danites can best be explained by the settlement of the Philistines. And it is suggestive that the first great champion to stand for Israel against the intruders, Samson, belonged to Zorah, whence went forth the Danite spies (Judg. xviii. 2).

The first allusion to the Philistines which we meet with in the Old Testament, that in the genealogical table of the nations in Genesis x, we have already discussed. Next we find a cycle of stories, told with but little variation both of Abraham and of Isaac (Gen. xx, xxi, xxvi), in which those heroes of old are brought into contact with a certain 'Abimelech, king of the Philistines'. In both cases the patriarch, to save himself, conceals his true relationship to his wife, which is revealed to the deceived monarch: in both, the latter displays a singular dignity and righteousness in the delicate position in which his guest's duplicity places him: and in both there is a subsequent dispute about the possession of wells. The stories are in short doublets of one another, and both echo a similar tale told of Abraham in Egypt, at an earlier stage of his career (Gen. xii). Whoever added the inept title to Psalm xxxiv evidently had these stories in his mind when he inadvertently wrote 'a Psalm of David when he changed his behaviour before *Abimelech*' instead of *Achish:* an unconscious reminiscence of the tale might possibly have been suggested by vv. 12, 13 of the Psalm in question.

The use of the word 'Philistine' in these stories has long been recognized as an anachronism. Perhaps with less harshness and equal accuracy we might characterize it as a rather free use of modern names and circumstances in telling an ancient tale. Even now we might find, for example, a popular writer on history saying that this event or that of the Early British period took place 'in Norfolk', although it is obvious that the territory of the North Folk must have received its Saxon name in later times. The tales of Abraham and Isaac were written when the land where their scenes were laid was in truth the Land of the Philistines; and the story-teller was not troubled with the question as to how far back that occupation lasted. Indeed when Abimelech first appears on the scene he is *not* a Philistine, but the Semitic king of the town of Gerar. The two passages in Gen. xxi, which might be understood 'they returned into [what we call] Philistia' . . . 'Abraham sojourned in [what is now] Philistia', have misled the writer (or copyist) of Gen. xxvi into supposing that Abimelech was actually king of the Philistines. In fact the Greek Version of xxvi. 8 seems to preserve an indication of older readings in which he was simply called, as in the other story, king of Gerar.

Noordtzij (*Filist.* p. 59) attempts to demonstrate a pre-Ramessu occupation of S. Palestine by the Philistines, principally on the ground that the time between Ramessu III and Samson or Saul is too short for the 'semitizing' process to have taken place. This seems hardly a cogent argument to me: the 'semitization' was by no means complete: the special Semitic rite of circumcision was not adopted: there is no reason to suppose that the language of the Philistines had been abandoned for a Semitic language. And we need have no difficulty in supposing such changes to take place with great rapidity. Thanks to the undermining influence of returned American emigrants, the Irish peasant has shown a change of attitude towards traditional beliefs in fairies and similar beings within the past twenty years as profound as any change that might have taken place between Ramessu III and Saul under the influence of the surrounding Semitic populations.

A similar anachronism meets us in Exodus xiii. 17, enshrining an ancient tradition that the ordinary caravan-route from Egypt by way of the coast was avoided in preference to the long and wearisome march through the desert, in order to keep clear of the Philistines and their military prowess. Likewise in the song preserved in Exodus xv, we find (v. 14) despondency attributed to the dwellers in Philistia at the news of the crossing of the Red Sea. This song, however, is probably not very ancient.

On the other hand, the writers who have contributed to the Pentateuch in its final form do not all share the indifference to chronological detail shown by the Yahwist story-teller. Often as are the tribes of Canaan enumerated in passages anticipatory of the conquest of the Promised Land, the Philistines are never mentioned: they have no share in the territory of the Hittite, the Girgashite, the Amorite, the Canaanite, and the Jebusite. In view of the prominence of the Philistines in the later history, this is a very significant fact. The solitary exception is so vague that it might almost be said to prove the rule—a reference to the Mediterranean sea by the name of 'the Sea of the Philistines' in Exodus xxxiii. 31. In Joshua xiii. 2, the 'districts' or 'circles' of the Philistines are enumerated among the places not conquered by the leader of the Hebrew immigration—the following verse, to which we shall return later, enumerates the 'districts'. But there is no reference to the Philistines in the parallel account contained in Judges i. There, in verse 19, the 'dwellers in the valley', i.e. in the low coast-land on which the Judahite territory bordered, are depicted as successfully resisting the aggression of the Hebrew tribe with the help of their iron chariots: the previous verse, which contradicts this, and which unhistorically claims that Judah captured the cities Gaza, Ashkelon, and Ekron, must necessarily be an interpolation. 1 In Judges iii. 3 we find an agreement with the passage just cited from Joshua—the five lords of the Philistines, as well as the 'Canaanites' (whatever may be exactly meant by the name in this connexion), the Phoenicians, and the Hi[tt]ites are enumerated as being left unconquered. The curious reason assigned, that this was to practise the Hebrews in war, is at any rate concordant with the old tradition that the terror of the warlike Philistines prevented the Hebrews following the direct route into the Promised Land.

The passages examined so far have rather been concerned with the settlement of the protagonists in the great struggle for the possession of Palestine than with the course of the struggle itself. We are to picture the Hebrew tribes crossing the Jordan from the East, and some little time afterwards the Philistines (and Zakkala) establishing themselves on the rich coast-lands: this much we can see with the aid of the Egyptian records cited in the preceding pages. We now follow the history of the conflict.

At the outset we are confronted by a puzzling group of passages. In the very ancient Song of Deborah, picturing the distracted state of the country under foreign oppressors, the writer describes how travellers and caravans, from fear, abandoned the main thoroughfares and journeyed along the by-paths, of which the winding valleys of Palestine offer an endless choice. This was in the days of a certain Shamgar son of Anath [1] (Judges v. 6). The name has a foreign appearance [2]: a Hittite analogy (Sangar) has been sought for it. We cannot, however, conclude that he was necessarily a foreigner, even though his progenitor is said to be Anath, which happens to be a well-known goddess-name. There is not another case of a Hebrew bearing so frankly idolatrous a name in the Old Testament. But in the Aswân papyri we have a glimpse of what Jewish life was, independent of priestly influences; and these show an extraordinary tolerance of heathen names and practices. We find Hosea son of Peti-Khnum. Names like 'Athar-ili, Nebonathan, Ben-Tirash occur in the community: the daughter of one Mahseiah swears in a law-court by the goddess Sati. Shamgar son of Anath would have been quite at home in this company.

The antecedent for this reference in Deborah's Song appears to lie in a verse at the end of chapter iii (v. 31), which says that Shamgar son of Anath killed six hundred Philistines with an ox-goad, and saved Israel. It is, however, obvious that this verse is out of place. It interrupts the flow of the narrative: there is no word of Philistine oppression in the context, and the text proceeds 'When *Ehud* was dead . . .' certain things happened, following on the story of Ehud which the Shamgar passage interrupts. The later development of the history contains no recognition of the labours of Shamgar. There are indeed few passages in literature which are so clearly no part of the original document: and we can hardly doubt that it has been inserted from some other source, or from another part of the book, in order to provide an explanation for the allusion in Deborah's Song.

It is curious that the chief Greek MSS. read Δίναχ instead of 'Anath' here, but not in Deborah's Song. [3] A number of Greek MSS. *repeat* the verse relating to Shamgar after xvi. 31—i.e. immediately after the story of Samson. This seems a better place for it. [4]

The Shamgar story, in short, looks like one of the floating traditions that have more particularly crystallized round Samson and the mighty men of David. A remarkable parallel to the exploit of Shamgar has been found in the deed of 'Shammah the Hararite'—a not dissimilar name—one of David's followers, who in some such rough and ready way defended a field of crops—barley or lentils—from Philistine marauders. [1]

But can the story be so summarily dismissed? Grant all the difficulties—that Shamgar's name has a foreign aspect, that the prose account of him is an interpolation, that the Philistines seem to appear too early on the scene; yet the scanty allusion to this obscure champion may after all record a tradition of the beginnings of the great struggle.

For besides Shamgar, Deborah's Song mentions another arresting personality. The very grandeur of the paean throws a romantic halo round the person of the unfortunate Sisera, victim of a crime against the desert law of hospitality difficult to parallel even in the wild annals of Bedawin life. The heartless glee with which the poet triumphs over the chieftain's anxious, watching mother makes the latter for us one of the most pathetic figures in the whole crowded gallery of the Old Testament. Time has brought its revenge for both mother and son.

In the prose version of the combat, Sisera is represented as the general of Jabin, king of Hazor, and the latter is the head of the attack on Israel. But Jabin has an altogether secondary place in the narrative, and Sisera is the central figure. Jabin, indeed, is probably imported into the story from the source that lies at the back of Joshua xi, where there is no mention of Sisera. In Psalm lxxxiii. 9 Sisera is mentioned before Jabin. He has a town of his own, 'Harosheth of the Gentiles,' more than a day's journey from the city of Jabin; and the vignette of his mother surrounded by her court ladies gives us a picture of a more important establishment than that of a mere captain of a host. Sisera in short is an independent king, and the story as we have it is either an account of a single campaign in which two kings were in league, or, more probably, a combination of the narratives of two campaigns wholly independent.

Harosheth is generally identified with the modern Harathiyeh, in the bottle-neck which forms the mouth of the plain of Esdraelon—a region entirely in Philistine hands, at least at the end of Saul's wars. This identification seems fairly trustworthy. Not far off from Harosheth was a village with the name Beth-dagon: and Harosheth itself is distinguished by the appellation 'of the gōyīm' or foreigners. In Joshua xii. 23 'the king of the gōyīm in Gilgal' is mentioned in noteworthy juxtaposition with Dor, which figures so conspicuously in the report of Wen-Amon; but this passage has been suspected and various emendations suggested, chief of which is to read לילגל for לגלגל and to translate 'king of nations belonging to Galilee'. This is of course reminiscent of the famous 'Galilee of the Gentiles' [1]; but on the other hand we may compare גלילות תשלפ 'the Galilees of Philistia' in Joshua xiii. 2 and Joel iii. 4 (= Hebrew iv. 4), which in the latter passage is mentioned immediately after the Philistine territory. The word gōyīm is of no more specific meaning than our word 'nations': though usually applied to foreigners, it may even on occasion be applied to the nation of Israel: so it cannot be said to be very conclusive. But one wonders whether in such passages and phrases as these it might not bear the special meaning of the foreigners par excellence, the most outlandish people with whom the Hebrews came into contact—that is to say the Philistines and their cognate tribes, for whom the Greek translators reserve the name ἀλλόφυλοι. In the present case they would more especially be the Zakkala, of whom Wen-Amon tells us, but who are not mentioned by name in the Hebrew writings.

Sisera's enormous host of iron chariots, a possession which, as we saw, also enabled the coast-dwellers of the South to hold their own, is emphasized in the prose account of the battle, as in the speech put by Deborah's Song into his mother's mouth: and it is interesting to notice that we hear again of these iron chariots as being on the plain of Esdraelon (Joshua xvii. 16).

The name of the prince also is suggestive. It is not Semitic: and the numerous Hittite names ending in *sira*—Khetasira and the like—have been quoted to indicate its possible origin. But we should not forget Badyra, the Zakkala prince of the neighbouring town of Dor. And may it not be asked whether Sisera, ארסיס, could be a reduplicated form derived from the root of זרס *seren* (the latter being possibly a participle), the one word of the Philistine language which we certainly know—the technical term for the 'lords of the Philistine state? This guess presupposes that the language of the Philistines was Indo-European—an assumption which it has not yet been possible either to prove or disprove. Some possible evidence of reduplication is afforded by such combinations as REREIET and perhaps KRKOKLES in the Praesos inscriptions. It is interesting to note that the name *Beneṣasira* occurs in the list of Keftian names on the Egyptian tablet described on a previous page.

If Sisera was a Philistine or at least one of cognate race, we have some use for Shamgar and his ox-goad. Otherwise, the latter must be expunged from the list of Judges, if he be not actually numbered among the oppressors, as Moore in his Commentary is inclined to do. The combination ANAIT, which ends one of the Praesos inscriptions just mentioned, has been compared to the name of Shamgar's parent Anath; but there is no probability that such a coincidence between a short inscription on the one hand, and a few proper names on the other, is of any importance.

In Judges x. 6, 7, 11 there is mention of Philistine oppression, in strange and scarcely intelligible connexion with the Amorites. This passage does not help us nearer to the solution of problems. It is in the narrative of Samson that the Philistines first come conspicuously on the scene. It is unnecessary to summarize the familiar incidents: indeed for our purpose these chapters, though of the deepest interest, are disappointing. The narrator is content to tell his tale, without troubling himself about the attendant circumstances which we would so gladly know.

In discussing this remarkable series of episodes it is unnecessary to raise the question of their historicity.[1] Still more irrelevant would be a discussion of the pseudo-scientific hypothesis that Samson (like Achilles, Heracles, Max Müller, Gladstone, and other demonstrated characters of mythology) was a solar myth. It is sufficient for the purpose of our present discussion that the tale gives us an early tradition of the condition of affairs at the time indicated; and as I have said elsewhere,[2] it is probably to be regarded as a prose epic concentrating into the person of a single ideal hero the various incidents of a guerrilla border-warfare.

This being postulated, one or two points of importance strike us in reading the story. The first is, that the Philistine domination was complete, and was passively accepted by the Hebrews. 'The Philistines are rulers over us' say the men of Judah, who propose to betray the champion to his enemies. As is so often the case with a nation of separate clans, even the pressure of a formidable common enemy cannot always heal their mutual jealousies. Ireland, in the face of the Vikings in the ninth century, and of the English in the twelfth, offers an instructive parallel. Only a chapter or two before the appearance of Samson, we have the distracting episode of Abimelech: a chapter or two later comes the story of the massacre of the Benjamites by the other tribes: and whatever may be the true chronological relationship of these narratives to the historical setting of the Samson epic, they at least indicate that there was a long period of inter-tribal disunion that would make it easy for a well-organized military nation to gain complete domination over the country.

But it was no mere military domination. The Philistines were accompanied by their wives and daughters, and the attractiveness of the latter in the eyes of Samson is a leading motive of his story. On this side of the narrative, however, there is one point to be noticed. There is no reason for branding the Philistines with the stigma of having produced the mercenary traitress Delilah: indeed, whatever indications there may be in her story point in an exactly opposite direction. Had tradition called her a Philistine, like Samson's first wife, the author of Judges would hardly have failed to make it clear. She is described as a woman in the Valley of Sorek; which, if it be the modern Wady es-Surâr, as is generally agreed, was partly in Israelite territory. Moreover, it would scarcely have been necessary for the Philistine lords to have offered the gigantic bribe of 1,100 pieces of silver each, to a woman of their own nation, that she might betray to them the arch-enemy of her race: it would be much more likely that they would use the persuasive argument of threatening her with the fate of her unlucky predecessor. The name appears again as that of a member of the tribe of Judah, in a genealogical fragment in 1 Chronicles iv. 19, preserved by the Greek Version, but lost from the Hebrew *textus receptus*. It is not too much to say that if the Delilah episode be read carefully, the various steps become more natural and intelligible when we picture the central figure as a tribeswoman of the men of Judah, who in the previous chapter had attempted to anticipate her act of betrayal.

It is noteworthy that nowhere in the Samson story is there any hint that there was a barrier of language between Hebrew and Philistine. Samson and his Philistine friends at Timnah exchange their rough jests without any difficulty; Delilah, whatever her race, converses with equal ease with the Philistine lords and with her Hebrew husband. The same point is to be noticed throughout the subsequent history, with the curious and significant exception of the very last reference to the Philistines in the historical books. Indeed, it has often been observed that the services of an interpreter are but rarely called for in the Old Testament: although it is possible that such an intermediary was sometimes used without the fact being specifically stated. ₁ But probably in ancient as in modern Palestine everybody who had any position at all to maintain could speak several languages. The officers of Hezekiah and Sennacherib, for instance, could understand each the other's tongue, and could pass from one to the other with the enviable ease of a modern Levantine polyglot.

The incident of Samson's hair has often been compared to the purple hair of Nisus, plucked out by Scylla at the instigation of Minos; and to the story of Pterelaos of Taphos and his golden hair given him by Poseidon, which rendered him immortal. Both stories are to be found in that endless mine, the *Bibliotheca* of Apollodorus. The connexion of *Minos* with the former story is noteworthy. It has, I believe, been suggested (but I have no note of the reference) that the story of the virtue inherent in Samson's locks may have been actually received by the Hebrews from Philistine sources. It may be merely a coincidence that the name of Samson's father, Manoah, resembles the name Minos.

Lastly, we notice in the Samson epic that as seen through Hebrew eyes the Philistines had already the three characteristics that marked them out from the other nations round about. The adjective 'uncircumcised', obviously the current term of abuse in all generations, already makes its appearance. Their peculiar government by 'lords' also meets us, but as it happens no particular 'lord' is named, nor does the Samson story give us any idea of their number. Thirdly, in the final scene, we are introduced to the mysterious Dagon, the chief deity of the Philistine pantheon.

For how long the Philistine domination lasted we have no means of knowing. There is no indication of the length of time supposed to elapse between the death of Samson and the appearance on the scene of Samuel. Eli, the priest of the High Place at Shiloh, may or may not have been contemporary with Samson: he appears suddenly on the scene as a man in extreme old age 'who had judged Israel forty years', and vanishes almost immediately.

The next stage of the history shows us the disunited and mutually hostile tribes of Israel gradually welding together under the pressure of their formidable enemy, and slowly but surely, though with more than one serious set-back, reversing the situation.

We begin with the unlucky battle in which for a time the Ark was lost (1 Sam. iv). The topography of the battle is uncertain: the Philistines pitched at a place quite unknown, Aphek, the Israelites at a spot of equally obscure topography, Eben-ezer, where Samuel afterwards set up a memorial pillar (vii. 12). The Philistines were the victors, and the Israelites attempted to turn the battle by fetching their national palladium from its resting-place in Shiloh. The Philistines were at first stricken with a superstitious fear; but recovering themselves they made a complete slaughter of the Israelites, and captured the Ark itself. Their rallying-cry 'Be strong and be men, that ye be not slaves to the Hebrews as they have been to you' corroborates, from the Philistine side, the evidence that the Philistines were the masters of the Hebrews at the time.

Now begins that strange story of the wanderings of the Ark. It would be natural to lay up the symbol of the deity of a vanquished people in the temple of the chief god of the conquerors: as Mesha laid up his religious trophies before Chemosh, so the Ark was deposited in the temple of Dagon at Ashdod—a temple of which we hear down to the time of the Maccabees (1 Macc. x. 84). But Dagon twice falls prostrate before the Ark, the second time being broken by the fall. At the same time a plague of mice or rats spread over the Philistine plain. There was a very similar plague over the same district in 1904, and enormous damage was done to the growing crops. Indeed, the peasants, whose fields were robbed almost as though by the prophet Joel's locusts, were reduced to tracking out the rat-holes and collecting the grain that the animals had brought down and stored: it was a curious sight to watch the women patiently engaged in this weary work, and gradually filling bags with the precious seed thus recovered. But in the Philistine experience the plague of rats had a yet more serious consequence. Not only did they 'mar the land', but as we now know to be the natural course of events, the parasites of the mice communicated to the people the disease of bubonic plague. [1]

The disease broke out first in Ashdod, and was naturally explained as due to the presence of the Ark. They therefore dispatched it to Gath, and of course the bearers carried the plague bacilli with them: again it was sent to Ekron, and again the plague was carried thither; and as the Philistines, even before they had secured their costly prize, had associated it with outbreaks of pestilence in Egypt (1 Sam. iv. 8), they easily connected it with their own troubles. How they returned it to Beth-Shemesh, and how the bacilli (carried probably by parasites on the kine, or perhaps on the coverings of the Ark) proved to be still virulent to the cost of the villagers who too rashly approached, are tales too well known to need repetition.

It is interesting that the Philistines sent back with the Ark votive models of their twofold plague, which yet was one, as their ancestors had been wont to do when, in search of healing from the ills of human flesh, they visited the Dictaean Cave in the ancient homeland.

The following chapter (vii) apparently represents a different strand of tradition. According to this the Ark was suffered to remain in Kiriath-Jearim no less than twenty years, until, probably, it was brought up to Jerusalem at the beginning of the reign of David. [1] Samuel held a reconciliation service, as it might be called, in which Israel renounced the various strange gods they had adopted. The Philistines came up to plunder this peaceful assembly, but were driven back by an appalling thunderstorm. The people gave chase, and smote the invaders to the unknown place called Beth-Car, to which reference has been made in the previous chapter; and a great memorial stone was set up at or near the spot where the Ark had been captured. We are then told that the Philistines restored certain cities, including Ekron and Gath (or according to the Greek text, Ashkelon and 'Azob', i.e. Gaza or Ashdod), to the Israelites, and that they never again came up to invade Israel.

It is noticeable that the narrator, with all his desire to glorify Samuel, avoids making a purely military leader of him, while emphasizing his religious functions. The victory is ascribed more to the thunderstorm, which is an answer to the 'whole burnt offering' offered by Samuel, than to military skill on the part of the Israelites or of any leader. The writer's patriotic enthusiasm (and perhaps some such record as Judges i. 18) have betrayed him into exaggeration with regard to the 'restoration' of cities that in fact had never been Israelite. But with regard to his conclusion 'that the Philistines never again invaded Israel', it is quite possible to judge him too harshly. If the Philistines were confined to the narrow strip of territory from Joppa southward, the statement would be absurd: but we have now seen that, at the time, the suzerainty of the Philistines over the whole of Palestine was complete, and that in all probability they actually occupied the *Northern* coast, the plain of Esdraelon as far as the Jordan, and even penetrated up the fertile valleys that wind through the Judaean mountains. This being so it may well be that the incident here recorded was actually the last case of *aggression;* but that in all the other cases in which the Philistines 'came up to war' the purpose was *defensive*, to meet Israelite encroachments on their territory. The passage therefore is not necessarily so 'extravagant' as some critics have made out.

However, there can be little doubt that the desire of the Hebrew people for a king, which now began to express itself, was the natural outcome of the growing sense of unity which under the pressure of the Philistine domination was rapidly developing. A leader was urgently needed who should be free from the specifically religious duties to which Samuel was entirely devoted; it was hoped that one who could thus give his whole attention to military matters might ultimately rid the people of the yoke that daily became more and more intolerable. Authorities differ as to how Samuel was affected by the popular demand. In one version he indignantly condemned it as a revolt against the theocracy of which he himself was at once Emperor and Pope. In another version he raised no objection to the new departure, definitely recognized it as a step towards delivery from the Philistines (1 Sam. ix. 16), chose the king and received him courteously, and declared to him the signs that testified to his election. From this programme we learn incidentally that the Philistines had a sort of *mudir* or governor at a place called Gibeah of God (probably to be identified with the modern village of Ram Allah about twelve miles north of Jerusalem). [1] This fact underlines, so to speak, what has already been said about the absence of Philistine aggressions after the battle of Beth-Car. With an outpost so far east as the spot indicated, the actual territory of the Philistines included all the places where fighting took place.

Saul assumed the kingdom, and immediately the first Israelite aggression took place: Jonathan slew the Philistine governor of Geba, where, as at Gibeah, there seems to have been a Philistine *mudir*.

The Philistines, rightly considering this a sign of revolt, came up to quell the insurrection. The Israelites were gathered together with Saul in Michmash, [2] but when they saw the overpowering might of the Philistines swooping down upon then) they hid themselves in the caves with which the country abounds. Saul waited anxiously for Samuel, and at last ventured himself to offer the necessary sacrifices: the denunciation, with which the stern old prophet expressed his resentment at this usurpation of his priestly functions, was apparently the first shock that disturbed Saul's delicately poised mental equilibrium, and paved the way for the insanity by which he was afterwards afflicted.

Jonathan again came to the rescue. With his armour-bearer he showed himself to the Philistines encamped at Michmash. They called to him to 'come up and see something'—note again that difference of language was no bar to intercourse—and the two young men, who had previously agreed to take such an invitation as an omen, climbed up to the camp. In some way they succeeded in throwing the camp into confusion, as Gideon had done with the Midianites. Soon the Philistines broke into a panic, which a timely earthquake intensified, and before long they were in flight, with the armies of Israel in hot pursuit. It is a remarkable story, and still more remarkable is the pendant—the tabu put by Saul on food, which had the natural result of making the victory less complete: the unconscious violation of the tabu by Jonathan: the consequent silence of the Divine oracle: his trial and condemnation: his redemption, no doubt by the substitution of another life: the pouring out of the blood when the tabu came to an end—all these are pictures of ancient religious custom and belief of the highest value.

The familiar story of the battle of Ephes-Dammim, with its central incident—the duel of David and Goliath—is the next scene in the drama. For the present, however, we pass it over: it is involved in a host of difficulties. Whatever view may be taken of the story, as we have it, it is evident that neither the spirit nor the power of the Philistines was broken by the rout at Michmash, but that they were able to meet Israel again soon after David's introduction to the court of Saul. David distinguished himself so as to arouse the jealousy of Saul, now rapidly falling into the morbid mental state that clouded his last days; and to that jealousy was due the exile of David in the wilderness.

With a madman's cunning, Saul at first attempted to work David's destruction by guile: he bribed him with the offer of his daughter's hand to go and bring him proof that he had slain a hundred of the uncircumcised—the trick was not unlike that which in later years David himself played on Uriah the Hittite. David, however, was more fortunate than his own victim, and fulfilled the task imposed on him.

But Saul's jealousy still pursued him, and he became a complete outlaw. His life during this period as narrated consists of a series of episodes, more or less disconnected. On one occasion he goes to the sanctuary at Nob, on the slope of the Mount of Olives (as we learn from Isa. x. 32), and takes the sword of Goliath thence to serve him as a weapon: we are then surprised to find him fleeing with this equipment to Gath, of all places—but probably the two incidents should not follow consecutively. At Gath he is recognized, and to avoid unpleasant consequences feigns insanity. This affliction would in Semitic circles secure him a measure of inviolability—the uncanny manifestations of mental derangement or degeneracy being curiously mixed up with notions of 'holiness'. But Achish, the dignified though simple-minded lord of Gath, was not a Semite, and had no such superstitions. He is almost modern in his protests—'If you see a madman, why do you bring him to me? I want no madmen about me, and I will not have him in my house!' 1 We almost hear an echo of the sarcasms of Zakar-Baal.

All through the story of David's outlawry raids of the Philistines run like a thread: and it must then, if never before, have been impressed upon him that when he came into his kingdom his first care must be to crush these troublesome neighbours finally and for ever. Now we read of his band saving the threshing-floors of Keilah from Philistine marauders: soon afterwards a Philistine raid breaks off negotiations between Saul and the men of Ziph for the betrayal of David.

But at last David, in despair of ever effecting a reconcilement with the insane Hebrew king, threw in his lot with the Philistines. Once more he comes to Gath—or, rather, we have probably a second version of the one incident, omitting the essential detail of the feigned madness. Here he was safe from Saul: but he did not stay very long. Probably (as in the previous version of the story) he found Gath uncomfortable as a place of residence, with his record of Philistine slaughter. So in Oriental wise he dissembled, and, flattering the king by pretending to be unworthy of living in the same city with him, he persuaded him to purchase his vassalage by putting Ziklag at his disposal. From this centre he raided various Bedawin camps, and, presenting the booty to his new master, he pretended that he had been attacking his own people. Thereby he gained the confidence of Achish, and no doubt acquired much serviceable information about Philistine military methods and resources.

Meanwhile the tragedy of Saul was working to its close. The Philistines were preparing for a final blow that would wipe off their recent reverses. Achish wished David, whom he blindly trusted, to accompany him as leader of his body-guard; but in this his wiser colleagues overruled him. They had already learnt, in the battle of Michmash, that the Hebrews that were with the Philistines' were not to be trusted when the battle went against their masters (1 Sam. xiv. 21). So Achish sent David away, with a dignified courtesy which contrasts pleasingly with the duplicity, not to say treachery, of his protégé. 1 David accordingly departed to his own quarters, and while the battle of Gilboa was being won and lost he was kept busy in avenging the raid which during his absence the Bedawin had very naturally made on Ziklag.

The armour of the dead Saul was hung in the house of Ashtoreth, and his body was fastened on the wall of Beth-Shan, the modern Beisan—a place close to the banks of the Jordan. This further corroborates the conclusion already indicated as to the wide extension of Philistine territory. For they would hardly have put the trophy where they could not reasonably have expected to retain it. 2

For the seven years of David's reign in Hebron the Philistines gave him no trouble. No doubt he continued to acknowledge himself as vassal of Achish, or of the Philistine oligarchy at large. Meanwhile Ish-baal (Ish-bosheth), Saul's son, guided and directed by Abner, set up a kingdom across Jordan, with its centre at Mahanaim: and the land of Ephraim remained subject to the Philistines. In the last two years of Ish-baal's life he extended his kingdom, doubtless under Philistine suzerainty, to Ephraim as well: an arrangement terminated by the defection of Abner to David and by his own assassination. This event left the way open for David to enlarge his borders, and to unite under his single sway the discordant elements of Judah and Ephraim. The ever-vigilant foes, not being willing to tolerate so large an increase in the strength of a subordinate, then came up against him. 1

Three battles, disastrous to the Philistines, are recorded as taking place early in David's reign over the united kingdoms. But the accounts of them are scanty and confused, and require careful examination. The following are the outline accounts of them which the author of the Book of Samuel transmits:

A. *The Battle of Baal-Perazim.*

And when the Philistines heard that they had anointed David king over Israel, all the Philistines went up to seek David; and David heard of it, and went down to the hold. 2 Now the Philistines had come and spread themselves in the valley of Rephaim. And David inquired of Yahweh, saying, Shall I go up against the Philistines? Wilt thou deliver them into mine hand? And Yahweh said unto David, Go up: for I will certainly deliver the Philistines into thine hand. And David cane to Baal-Perazim, and David smote them there; and he said, Yahweh hath broken mine enemies before me, like the breach of waters. Therefore he called the name of that place Baal-Perazim. And they left their images there, and David and his men took them away.'—2 Samuel v. 17-21.

B. *The Battle of Geba.*

'And the Philistines came up yet again, and spread themselves in the valley of Rephaim. And when David inquired of Yahweh, he said, Thou shalt not go up: make a circuit behind them, and come upon them over against the balsams. And it shall be, when thou hearest the sound of marching in the tops of the balsams, that then thou shalt bestir thyself: for then is Yahweh gone out before thee to smite the host of the Philistines. And David did so, as Yahweh commanded him; and smote the Philistines from Geba until thou come to Gezer.'—2 Samuel v. 22–25.

C. *The Battle of (?)*

'And after this it came to pass, that David smote the Philistines, and subdued them: and David took (   ) out of the hand of the Philistines.'—2 Sam. viii. 1. These outlines may to some small extent be filled in from other sources. The priestly writer of Chronicles is careful to add to the account of the first battle that the idols of the Philistines, captured after the rout, were burnt with fire (1 Chron. xiv. 8–12). The site of Baal-Perazim is unknown. It seems to be mentioned again in Isaiah xxviii. 21, in connexion with Gibeon: perhaps this passage refers to the first two battles. In the account of the second battle the Chronicler likewise substitutes Gibeon for Geba (1 Chron. xiv. 13–16): while in the third, instead of an unintelligible expression in the version of Samuel, he has 'David took Gath and her towns out of the hand of the Philistines' (xviii. 1).

Among these battles must probably be fitted some scraps of biography that now find a place much later both in Samuel and in Chronicles. They are confused and corrupt, but are to the effect that at certain specified places, certain Philistine champions were slain by certain of the mighty men of David.

The first is the familiar tale of David and Goliath, which we passed over a while ago, and which cannot be dissociated from these fragments. David is sent by his father to the battle-field of Ephes-Dammim, to bring supplies to his elder brothers. His indignation is roused by a gigantic Philistine champion named Goliath of Gath, who challenges the Israelites to provide one who shall fight with him and decide the battle by single combat. The champion is minutely described: he was somewhere between nine and eleven feet high, with a helmet, a coat of mail weighing 5,000 shekels, greaves and a javelin, all of bronze, as well as an iron-pointed spear like a weaver's beam. How David, though a youth unable to wear armour, goes against the giant, exchanges taunting speeches with him, and brings him down with his sling, are tales too familiar to rehearse (1 Sam. xvii).

The difficulties of the passage are many. The inconsistency of David, already (ch. xvi. 21) the armour-bearer of Saul, being now totally unknown to him, has been a crux to the harmonists of all generations: though this difficulty is evaded by an important group of the Greek MSS., which omit bodily verses xvii. 12–31, 55–xviii. 5—that is, everything inconsistent with David's being already at court and known to Saul. The omitted verses are probably fragments of another parallel narrative. But even then we are not quite free from troubles. The whole machinery of the ordeal by duel recalls incidents of the Trojan war, or the tale of the Horatii and Curiatii, rather than what we are accustomed to look for in Semitic warfare; David's improbable flight to Gath soon after the battle has already been commented upon; and, as will presently be seen, we possess another account of the battle of Ephes-Dammim, which is quite inconsistent with the Goliath story, and, indeed, leaves no room for it.

The second fragmentary narration is unfortunately found in Samuel only (2 Sam. xxi. 15–17). It reads 'And the Philistines had war again with Israel; and David went down, and his servants with him, and fought against the Philistines: and David waxed faint. And (a champion) which was of the sons of Rapha, the weight of whose spear was 300 (shekels) of bronze in weight, he being girded with a new [*word lost*], thought to have slain David. But Abishai the son of Zeruiah succoured him and smote the Philistine and killed him. Then the men of David sware unto him, saying, "Thou shalt go no more out with us to battle, that thou quench not the lamp of Israel."'

The rendering 'a champion' is suggested for the unintelligible בנב ישבו, treated as a proper name 'Ishbi-benob' in the English version. As it stands it means 'and they dwelt in Nob', which clearly makes no sense; and the emendation that is most current—by the change of one letter, turning *Nob* to *Gob*, and moving the phrase so as to follow 'and his servants with him' in the previous sentence—is not altogether satisfactory. For 'Gob' itself is probably, as we shall see, corrupt; and it is hard to see how the sentence could have been transposed from a place where it makes passable sense to a place where it makes complete nonsense. The reading here suggested is איש־הבינם, literally 'man of the betweens', apparently a technical term for a champion, which is actually applied to Goliath in 1 Samuel xvii. Though differing in detail, and transmitted in a garbled form, the general resemblance of the description of the equipment of this warrior to that of Goliath is too striking to be overlooked; and we are thus led to wonder whether this may not be a version of the Goliath story in which the issue of the duel was very nearly the reverse of that in the familiar narrative. One is also tempted to ask whether in the 'oath' of the men of David (for which compare 2 Sam. xviii. 3) we are to see an explanation of David's having stayed in Jerusalem while Joab was acting for the king in his operations against the Ammonites, with the disastrous consequence of the episode of Bath-Sheba. If this oath is to be literally understood, this incident of the champion slain by David's nephew must belong to the end of David's operations against the Philistines, all of which seem to have been directed by the king in person.

The third fragment appears in both 2 Samuel and 1 Chronicles. The Samuel version says 'And it came to pass after this, that there was again war with the Philistines at Gob: then Sibbecai the Hushathite slew Saph, which was of the sons of Rapha. And there was again war with the Philistines at Gob; and Elhanan the son of Jaare-oregim the Beth-lehemite slew Goliath the Gittite, the staff of whose spear was like a weaver's beam' (2 Sam. xxi. 18, 19).

In the parallel account (1 Chron. xx. 4), Gezer is substituted for Gob, Sippai for Saph, Jair for Jaare-oregim, and 'slew Lahmi the brother of Goliath 'for the Beth-lehemite slew Goliath'.

With regard to the first of these divergencies, it should be noticed that the place-name 'Gob' is not mentioned elsewhere. Following Clermont-Ganneau I was formerly inclined to accept *Gezer* as the correct reading—the change would be easy, גזר for גב—but I now see two formidable difficulties. In the first place, it is not likely that the well-known place-name Gezer would be corrupted to a name utterly unknown: in the second, the name 'Gob' is written בג in both places, without the *mater lectionis* which the emendation suggested requires. Noting that in the text in Samuel the name 'Gob' is in both places followed by a word beginning with the letter ע, I would now suggest that a second ע has dropped out in both places, and that for Gob we are to read גבע, Geba. 1 The advantage of this correction is, that it would make both the Samuel and Chronicles versions right, and would show us where to fit the fragment under discussion. For we can scarcely avoid connecting an incident, said in one version to take place at Geba, and in another version at Gezer, with a battle which is definitely stated to have begun in one of these two places and finished in the other. The deaths of Saph and of Goliath therefore took place in the second of the three battles enumerated above (p. 53).

The other divergencies need not detain us so long. The question of the spelling of the champion's name is scarcely important: yet it is tempting to inquire whether the form in Chronicles, ספי, is not to be preferred, and, further, whether it may not be that it actually finds an echo to this day in the commonplace Arabic name *Tell eṣ-Ṣāfi*, commonly rendered 'The clear mound', 2 whereby the most probable site of ancient Gath is now known. Jair for Jaare-oregim is certainly right, the latter half of the name as given by Samuel being a dittography of the word 'weaver's beam' in the next line; on the other hand, the Chronicler's evolution of Goliath's brother Lahmi out of the name of Jair's native place is obviously some scribe's attempt to get rid of an evident harmonistic difficulty.

The fourth fragment follows the last in both places. 'And there was again war at Gath, where was a man of great stature, that had on every hand six fingers, and on every foot six toes, four and twenty in number; and he also was born to Rapha. And when he defied Israel, Jonathan the son of Shimei David's brother slew him. These four were born to Rapha in Gath; and they fell by the hand of David, and by the hand of his servants.' The Chronicler's version is substantially identical.

Let us now try to dovetail these seemingly incoherent fragments into a consistent narrative. Nearly all of them will be found to hang together with a logical connexion between them. We begin with the story of Jesse sending David as a youth to his brothers, and their surly reception of him, in *some* campaign. This story, though, as we have seen, it almost makes nonsense of the place where it is found, is so graphic and circumstantial that it cannot lightly be thrown aside. It is not improbable, however, that it was by his musical rather than his military ability that he attracted attention on this occasion, and was brought to the notice of Saul and Jonathan (1 Sam. xvi. 14–18, xviii. 1). At first he was received kindly, and made Saul's armour-bearer.

Then came the battle of Ephes-Dammim, the full account of which is lost. But by combining 2 Samuel xxiii. 9 with 1 Chronicles xi. 13, two mutilated but complementary passages, we can gain some idea of what happened. The Philistines came up to battle at Ephes-Dammim; the men of Israel fled; but David, aided by Eleazer the son of Dodo the Ahohite (whatever that may mean), held them 'in the valley between Shocoh and Azekah' and fought till their hands clave to their swords. They succeeded in turning the victory, and the people came back 'only to spoil'. Well might the maidens, after such an exhibition of valour, sing that 'Saul had slain thousands but David had slain myriads'. The folk-tale of a giant-killing shepherd-boy, coloured by some actual incident of David's later campaigns, has been substituted for the less picturesque story of the battle: a relic of the excised part may possibly be seen in the verse inserted after 1 Samuel xix. 7: 'And there was war again: and David went out, and fought with the Philistines, and slew them with a great slaughter; and they fled before him.' And when the tribes of Israel came to David to make him king, they remind him that even in Saul's lifetime it was he who used to lead them out to war (2 Sam. v. 2).

The triumph-song of the women roused the jealousy of Saul, and he drove David into exile. The other tales of Philistine routs, which meet us in the lists of David's mighty men, appear to relate to the time of the outlawry. Shammah's defence of the lentil-field, to which reference has already been made, was of the same order as the repulse of the raid on the threshing-floor of Keilah: the breaking through the Philistine camp at Rephaim by the three heroes, in quest of the Bethlehem water, is definitely assigned to the Adullam period. Finally David took service in Gath, and became thoroughly acquainted with that important city.

When the kingdoms of Judah and Israel were united, the Philistines came to break up his power; and three engagements were fought, all disastrous to the hereditary enemies of the Hebrews. The first was the battle of Baal-Perazim, of which we have no particulars save the picture of a hurried flight in which even the idols were left behind. The second, that of Geba, is more interesting. The incident of the oracle of the sacred trees is one of the many noteworthy landmarks in Old Testament religion. The topography of the battle seems at first sight difficult to follow: but it works out easily when one knows the configuration of the ground. The valley or plain of Rephaim is usually equated with the broad expanse that lies south-west of Jerusalem. Geba was some four miles to the north of the city. What must have happened was, that David's men circled behind the Philistine camp, under cover, probably, of the hills to the west of the plain (now crowned by the Greek Patriarch's summer residence Kat'êmôn); that is, down the picturesque valley in which stands the Convent of the Cross. Then crossing into the Wady el-Werd by the site of the modern village of Malhah, 1 they attacked the Philistines on the rear. Finding their retreat (down the present Wady el-Werd and its western continuation, the Wady es-Surar) cut off; the Philistines fled northward, past Jerusalem, as far as the village of Geba, and then rushed down the valley of Aijalon, which opens out on the coast-plain not far from Gezer. Some time in this battle or the subsequent rout Sibbecai (or Mebunni) slew Saph, and Elhanan slew Goliath.

Contrary to most modern commentators I assume that this raid of the Philistines took place *after* (or perhaps *during*, which is not improbable) David's successful siege of Jerusalem. If David was still in Hebron at the time, I cannot conceive what the Philistines were doing in the valley of Rephaim. 'They would have come up one of the more southerly valleys to attack him.

Lastly took place the final and decisive victory which crushed for ever the Philistine suzerainty. The union at last effected among the tribes of Israel gave them a strength they had never had before; yet it is hard to understand the complete collapse of the people who had been all-powerful but a few years previously. W. Max Müller attempts to account for it 1 by an unrecorded attack of the Egyptian king, whereby he possessed himself of the Philistine coastland: arguing that in a list of Sheshonk's conquests in his campaign

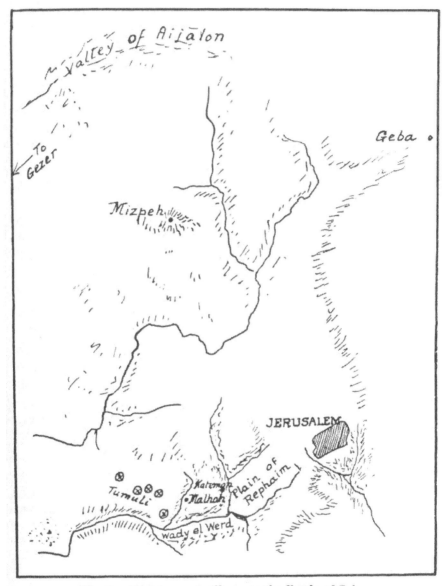

Fig. 2. Sketch-map to illustrate the Battle of Geba.

recorded in 1 Kings xiv. 25 no Philistine city is mentioned, for the simple reason that they must have been already in Egyptian hands. On this theory also he accounts for the capture of Gezer (an extension of the Egyptian territory) recorded in 1 Kings ix. 16.

The site of the last battle is successfully concealed under a hopeless corruption of the text. We are told in Samuel that David took *Metheg ha-ammah* out of the hand of the Philistines: a phrase that means 'bridle of the cubit' or 'of the metropolis', but defies convincing explanation or emendation. The old versions all presuppose an identical or similar text: Chronicles has 'Gath and her suburbs', which is probably a guess at a reading which should be at least intelligible. It cannot be right, for we find Gath still independent under its king Achish at the beginning of Solomon's reign (1 Kings ii. 39). [1] This, however, does not forbid our supposing the decisive battle to have taken place at or near Gath: a very likely place for David to attack, as he was no doubt familiar with its fortifications. There certainly appears to have been a battle at Gath where the unnamed polydactylous champion defied Israel and was slain by a nephew of David. Perhaps he was one and the same with the Gittite champion whom the English version calls Ishbi-benob, and from whom David, when hard pressed, was rescued likewise by one of his nephews. In this incident, on the theory here put forward, is the historical basis of the David and Goliath story. In this case 2 Samuel xxi. 22 ('these *four* were born to "the giant" in Gath') would be an editorial note.

Before leaving this record of the champions of the Philistines which we have thus endeavoured to put into order, we must notice that, strictly speaking, they are not to be classed as Philistines at all. The expression 'son of Rapha', translated 'giant' in the English version, implies rather that the family were of the remnant of the Rephaites or Anakim, the tall aboriginal race which the Israelites on their coming found established in Hebron and neighbouring villages, Gath, Gaza, and Ashdod. According to Joshua xi. 21 they were driven out utterly from the Hebron district, but a remnant was left in the Philistine towns, where no doubt they mingled with the western newcomers. The tall stature attributed to these 'champions'—a physical feature never ascribed in the history to the Philistines themselves [2]—fits in with this theory of the origin of the family. By Delilah and Goliath the Philistine nation is judged: but there is no proof that there was a drop of Philistine blood in either the one or the other.

The commentators agree that the ancient psalm incorporated in Psalm lx. (8–12) and cviii. (7–10) can be as old as David. If so, it may well have been a paean of the victory over the Philistines and the other neighbouring nations.

That the Philistine power was utterly broken is shown by the significant fact that in the distractions which vexed the later years of David—the revolt of Absalom and of Sheba—they made no effort to recover their lost ground. Quite the contrary: we are surprised to find David's body-guard consisting of 'Cherethites and Pelethites', Cretans and Phili(s)tines: a Gittite called Obed-Edom houses the ark when the ill-omened incident of Uzza had interrupted the first attempt to bring it to Jerusalem: and another Gittite, Ittai by name, was one of the few people who remained faithful to David when Absalom had stolen the hearts of his followers. So their ancient kinsmen the Shardanu appear, now as enemies, now as loyal mercenaries of Egypt. And in the later history, except a few halfhearted attempts like that in the time of Jehoram, the Philistines took no decisive advantage of the internal dissensions between Judah and Israel, or of their many struggles with the Syrians and other foreign foes. From the time of David their power, and indeed their very individuality, dwindle away with a rapidity difficult to parallel. The contrast between the pre-Davidic and the post-Davidic Philistines is one of the most extraordinary in human history.

But in Palestine the Philistines were, after all, foreigners: they had come from their healthy maritime life to the fever-haunted and sirocco-blasted land of Canaan. The climate of that country guards it for its Semitic heirs, and Philistine and Crusader alike must submit to the laws of human limitations.

The Philistine body-guard above referred to was perhaps organized during David's stay in Ziklag. In the later history some traces of the organization seem to survive. The 'Carites', as they are now significantly called, help Jehoiada to put down the usurping queen Athaliah. In Ezekiel (xliv. 7 sqq.) there is a prophecy against certain uncircumcised foreigners who are introduced, apparently in some official capacity, into the Temple: and in Zephaniah i. 8, 9 'those that are clothed with foreign apparel' and 'those that leap over the threshold' in the 'day of the Lord's sacrifice' are denounced. Though suggestive, neither of these passages is as clear as we should like: the possibility of there being some connexion between the threshold rite in Zephaniah and the analogous rite in the Temple of Ashdod (1 Sam. v. 5) has often been noticed. It is an interesting possibility—we cannot say more—that there actually was a Philistine body-guard round the king and his court at Jerusalem, and that the Temple itself, built as we shall see after a Philistine model, was protected by Philistine janissaries. This might explain the unexpected reappearance of the heathenish name of Sisera among the Nethinim or Temple servitors recorded in Ezra ii. 53, Nehemiah vii. 55.

Footnotes

40:1 See Moore's *Commentary*, p. 37.

41:1 The additional note of time, 'In the days of Jael', is generally rejected as a gloss.

41:2 See Moore's *Judges*, pp. 142, 143, and *Journal of American Oriental Society*, xix b, p. 159.

41:3 The name Shamgar is given as Σαμεγαρ, Σαμαγαρ, Σεμεγαρ, Σεμαγαρ, Αμεγαθ, Σαμεγαθ, Μαιγαρ, Εμεγαρ. His father's name in Judges iii is given as Διναχ, Δειναχ, Αναθ, Εναχ, Αιμαθ, Λιναθ; in Judges v as Αναθ, Κεναθ, Εναθ, Εναθαμ, Ανεθεμ.

41:4 The verse as repeated says that 'Semegar (or Emegar) son of Anan (Ainan, Enan) arose after Samson, and slew of the Foreigners, 600 men without the cattle, and he also saved Israel'. Note the transformation of the ox-goad.

42:1 2 Sam. xxiii. 11; 1 Chron. xi. 13.

43:1 Isa. ix. 1 (= Hebrew viii. 23).

44:1 For a study (from a conservative standpoint) of the historicity of the Samson narrative see Samson, eine Untersuchung des historischen Charakters von Richt. xiii–xvi, von Dr. Edmund Kalt, Freiburg i. Br., 1912. This brochure contains a very useful bibliography.

44:2 *A History of Civilization in Palestine*, p. 54.

46:1 Thus, it is only by a foot-note, as it were, that we learn that Joseph employed an interpreter in conversing with his brethren.

47:1 Some commentators (e. g. H. P. Smith in the *International Critical Commentary*), while recognizing that the disease was plague, have missed the essential significance of the mice, and would remove them altogether as 'late redactional insertion'. Although in the Hebrew received text, as reproduced in the English Bible, the 'mice' come in awkwardly as though a sudden afterthought, the Greek Version makes them much more prominent throughout the narrative; and there is no possible reason why any redactor (unless he had divined some of the most recent discoveries in bacteriology) should have introduced mice into the story at all. The distorted version of the plague which destroyed Sennacherib's army, recorded in Herodotus ii. 141, also introduces mice very conspicuously.

48:1 The data for the chronology of Saul's reign are notoriously insufficient. Note that Eli's great-grandson was priest in Shiloh at the time of the battle of Michmash (1 Sam. xiv. 3).

49:1 In the English version (1 Sam. x. 5) the word נציב, which in 1 Kings iv. 19 and elsewhere means 'a prefect or officer', is translated, probably wrongly, 'camp'.

49:2 There are some difficulties of interpretation and other critical complications in the passage, on which see the standard commentators.

51:1 The notion of a commentator, that Achish's protest was due to his being already troubled with insanity in his family, deserves a place in the same cabinet of curiosities with the speculations of the ancient blockhead who supposed that when Our Lord wrote with His finger on the ground (John viii. 6) He was making a catalogue of the secret sins of the bystanders!

52:1 No doubt there was a certain element of policy in Achish's hospitality: David being the known rival of the Hebrew king, it probably seemed desirable to foment the division between them. Winckler (*Gesch. Isr.*, p. 224) says (*ex cathedra!*) 'Was über Davids Aufenthalt an seinem Hofe gesagt wird, ist Fabel'. This sort of negative credulity is just as bad science as the positive credulity which swallows whole all the fancies of historical myth-makers.

52:2 Unless, indeed, we are to identify this Beth-Shan with the unknown 'Shen', mentioned in the corrupt passage 1 Sam. vii. 12.

53:1 For a discussion of the obscure period of the dual reign of David and Ish-baal, with special reference to the problem of the reconcilement of David's seven and a half years with Ish-bosheth's two years, see the important article by Kamphausen, *Philister and Hebräer zur Zeit Davids*, in *Zeitsch. f. d. alttest. Wissensch.* (1886, vi, p. 44.

53:2 Hardly Adullam, as some commentators have supposed. Did the Adullam life continue after David was anointed king on Hebron?

56:1 The Greek and Peshitta versions read *Gath*.

56:2 But really meaning, if anything, 'The mound of the clear one.' 'The clear mound' would be *Et-tell eṣ-Ṣāfa*.

58:1 They must in this case have passed close by some ancient tumuli, which stand west of Malhah: possibly the sacred balsam-trees were associated with these.

59:1 *Asien and Europa*, pp. 389, 390.

60:1 It is *possible* that David showed kindness to Achish, in return for the kindness he had received from him, and allowed him to continue in his kingdom under vassalage. But this is perhaps hardly probable: and evidently the runaway servants of Shimei thought that they would be out of their master's reach in Gath, so that that town was most likely quite independent of Jerusalem.

60:2 I may quote from *The Excavation of Gezer*, vol. i, p. 64, the descriptions of the only bones that have yet been found in Palestine which can be called 'Philistine' with reasonable probability. They 'are comparable with the types of ancient Cretan bones described by Duckworth and Hawes, and with Cretan bones in the Cambridge Museum. They represent a people of fairly tall stature (the man in grave 3 was 5′ 10″, that in grave 3 was 6′ 3½″). They were probably about or under 40 years of age. In all the femora were not pilastered and the tibiae not platycnemic. p. 61 The skulls were ellipsoidal, mesaticephalic, orthognathous, megaseme (with wide orbits), mesorrhine (with moderately wide nose), and microdont. The female skull in grave 4 was a little wider in proportion, and though the teeth were moderately small, the incisors projected forward, though not enough to make the face prognathous. The lower teeth were also very oblique.'

III. Their Decline and Disappearance.

A few simple figures will show the comparative insignificance into which the Philistines fell after their wars with David. In the first book of Samuel, the name 'Philistine' or 'Philistines' occurs 125 times. In the second book it occurs only twenty-four times, and some of these are reminiscent passages, referring to earlier incidents. In the two books of the Kings together the name occurs only six times.

Achish was still 'King of Gath', as we have already seen, at the beginning of Solomon's reign, and the coast] and strip was still outside Hebrew territory. Gezer was presented to Solomon's wife as a marriage portion. After the partition of the kingdom, Nadab son of Jeroboam I besieged Gibbethon, a now unknown Philistine village, where he was killed by his successor Baasha. The siege was apparently renewed at the end of Baasha's own reign, but why this village was made a centre of attack is a question as obscure as its topography. Ahaziah sent to consult the Oracle of Ekron. The Shunammite woman who had entertained Elisha sojourned during the seven years' famine in the land of the Philistines—a testimony to the superior fertility of that part of the country. Turning to the records of the southern kingdom, we learn from the Chronicler that certain of the Philistines brought presents and silver for tribute to Jehoshaphat: but that under his son Jehoram they revolted and carried away his substance. In the parallel version in Kings the revolt is localized in the insignificant town of Libnah. The great king Uzziah, on the other hand, broke the walls of Gath—which had probably been already weakened by the raid of Hazael of Syria (2 Kings xii. 18)—as well as the walls of Jabneh and of Ashdod, and established cities of his own in Philistine territory. This is the last we hear of the important city of Gath in history: henceforth it is omitted from the enumerations of Philistine cities in prophetic denunciations of the race. In the time of Ahaz there seems to have been a revival of the old spirit among the beaten people. Profiting by the Edomite raid which already harassed Judah, they took some cities from Southern Judah, including Beth-shemesh, Aijalon, Gederoth, Shocho, Timnath, and Gimzo, which are not elsewhere reckoned as Philistine property (2 Chron. xxviii. 18); certainly the first of these was a Hebrew village even at the time of the greatest extension of Philistine power. This 'Philistine revival' seems to have inspired Isaiah in a denunciation of Ephraim (Isa. ix. 12), but whether the invasion of the northern kingdom there threatened ever took place is not recorded. Probably not, as Hezekiah once more reversed the situation, smiting the Philistines as far as Gaza (2 Kings xviii. 8).

At this point we glean some welcome details of history from the annals of the Assyrian kings. Hadad-Nirari III (812–783) enumerates the Philistines among the Palestinian states conquered by him about 803 R. c., but enters into no particulars. Tiglath-Pileser III, however, (745–727) gives us fuller details. Rezōn (in the Hebrew Rezīn) of Syria, and Pekah of Samaria were in league, whereas Ahaz of Jerusalem had become a vassal of the king of Assyria. The Philistines had attached themselves to the Syrian league, so that in 734 B.C. Tiglath-Pileser came up with the special purpose of sacking Gaza. Ḥanunu, the king of Gaza, fled to Sebako, king of Egypt; but he afterwards returned and, having made submission, was received with favour. ₁

Some four years earlier Mitinti, king of Ashkelon, had revolted, trusting to the support of Rezon. But the death of Rezon so terrified the king that he fell sick and died—possibly he poisoned himself, knowing what punishment would be in store for him at the hands of the ferocious Assyrian. His son Rukipti, who reigned in his stead, hastened to make submission.

About 713 another Philistine city comes into prominence. This is Ashdod, the king of which, Azuri, refused to pay tribute and endeavoured to stir up the neighbouring princes to revolt. Sargon, king of Assyria (722–705), came down, expelled Azuri, and established in his stead his brother Aḥimiti. An attempt was made by the Philistines—Sargon's scribe calls them Hittites—to substitute one Yamani, who had no claim to the throne. But this bold usurper fled to the land of Meluḫḫa in N. Arabia when Sargon was on his way to the city. 1 These operations of Sargon against Ashdod are referred to in a note of time in Isaiah xx. 1.

The next king, Sennacherib (705–681), had trouble with the remnant of the Philistines. Mitinti's son Rukipti had been succeeded by his son Sarludâri, but it seems as though this ruler had been deposed, and a person called Zidka reigned in his stead. Sennacherib found conspiracy in Zidka, and brought the gods of his father's house, himself, and his family into exile to Assyria, restoring Sarludâri to his former throne, while of course retaining the suzerainty. In this operation he took the cities of Beth-Dagon, Joppa, Bene-Berak, and Azuri, which belonged to Zidka. These names still survive in the villages of Beit Dejan, Ibrak, and Yazur, in the neighbourhood of Jaffa.

At the same time the Ekronites had revolted against the Assyrian. Their king, Padi, had remained a loyal vassal to his overlord, but his turbulent subjects had put him in fetters and sent him to Hezekiah, king of Judah, who cast him into prison. The Ekronites summoned assistance from North Arabia and Egypt, and met Sennacherib in El-Tekeh. Here they were defeated, and Sennacherib marched against Ekron, slaying and impaling the chief officers. Padi was rescued from Jerusalem, his deliverance being no doubt part of the tribute paid by Hezekiah (2 Kings xviii. 14). Sennacherib then cut off some of the territory of Judah and divided it among his vassals, Mitinti, king of Ashdod, Padi the restored king of Ekron, and Zilbel, king of Gaza. 1

Sennacherib was assassinated in 681, and his son Esarhaddon (681–668) reigned in his stead. In the lists of kings in subjection to this monarch we find Mitinti, king of Ashkelon (the Assyrian records seem to confuse Ashkelon and Ashdod), and Zilbel, king of Gaza, of whom we have heard before. Padi has disappeared from Ekron, and to him has succeeded a king with the old Philistine name of Ikausu (= Achish). On the other hand a king with the Semitic name of Aḥimilki (Ahimelech) is king of Ashdod. All these kings survived into the reign of Assurbanipal, who began to reign in 668. 2

According to Jeremiah xlvii. 1 (not the Greek Version) 'Pharaoh smote Gaza' in the time of that prophet. This most likely was Necho, on his way northward when Josiah, with fatal consequences to himself, tried to check him. Herodotus is supposed to refer to this when he says (ii. 159) that Necho took a great city of Syria called 'Kadytis', which elsewhere (iii. 5) he describes as a city in his opinion not smaller than Sardis. It is a possible, but not a convincing, hypothesis, that Kadytis may represent some form of the name of Gaza. 1

Here the Assyrian records leave us. We have, however, one more Biblical reference, in the last paragraph of the book of Nehemiah, which is of very great importance (xiii. 23, 24). The walls of Jerusalem had been restored; the law published and proclaimed; all the steps had been taken to establish an exclusive theocratic state in accordance with the priestly legislation; when the leader was dismayed to discover certain Jews who had married women of Ashdod, of Ammon, and of Moab, the very communities that had put so many obstacles in the way of the work of restoration. 2 Not only so, but there were already children; and as is usual in such cases of mixed marriage, these children spoke the language of their mothers only. Nehemiah indulged in a passionate display of temper, treating the culprits with personal violence, and probably he compelled them to put away their wives, as Ezra did in a similar case. But the interest for us is not in Nehemiah's outburst, but in his reference to the speech of the children. They spoke half in the speech of Ashdod, and could not speak in the Jews' language. In spite of Sennacherib's transportations and deportations; in spite of the long and exhausting siege of twenty-nine years which the city (according to Herodotus ii. 157) sustained in the following century at the hands of Psammetichus; yet the ancient tongue of the Philistines lingered still in Ashdod, the town which probably retained exotic characteristics the longest. The distinction which Strabo (XVI. ii. 1) draws between the Γαζαῖοι and the Ἀζώτιοι ('Jews, Idumaeans, Gazaeans, and Azotii' being the four minor races of Syria which he enumerates) may possibly be founded on a reminiscence of these linguistic survivals. No doubt the language was by now much contaminated with Semitic words and idioms, but still it possessed sufficient individuality to be unintelligible without special study. It had of course lost all political importance, so that it was not as in the days of Samson and Jonathan, when every Hebrew of position was obliged to know something of the tongue of the powerful rivals of his people: it was now a despised *patois*, much as are the ancient Celtic languages in the eyes of the average Saxon. In the chatter of these little half-breeds the stern Jewish puritan was perhaps privileged to hear the last accents of the speech of Minos, whose written records still 'mock us, undeciphered'.

It is true that some critics have explained the 'speech of Ashdod' as being the tongue of Sennacherib's colonists. If so, however, Nehemiah (himself a returned exile from a neighbouring empire to Sennacherib's) would probably have had some understanding of it and of its origin, and would have described it differently. The Semitic speech of the children of the Ammonite and Moabite mothers does not seem to have caused him so much vexation.

In Gaza, too, Philistine tradition still survived. Down to the time of the Maccabean revolt there remained here a temple of Dagon, destroyed by Jonathan Maccabaeus (1 Macc. x. 83, 84; xi. 4). But these traditional survivals of religious peculiarities are mere isolated phenomena: apart from them the absorption of Philistia in the ocean of Semitic humanity is so complete that its people ceases to have an independent history. It were profitless to trace the story of Philistia further, through the campaigns of Alexander, the wars of the Maccabees and the Seleucids, the Roman domination, and the complex later developments: the record is no longer the history of a people; it is that of a country.

Nevertheless, the tradition of the Philistines still lives, and will continue to live so long as the land which they dominated three thousand years ago continues to be called 'Palestine', and so long as its peasant parents continue to tell their children their tales of the *Fenish*. One accustomed to the current English pronunciation of the name of the *Phoenicians* might for a moment be misled into supposing that these were the people meant: but the equation is philologically impossible. There can be no doubt that this people of tradition, supposed to have wrought strange and wonderful deeds in the land, to have hewn out its great artificial caves and built its castles and even the churches and monasteries whose fast-decaying ruins dots its landscape—that this people is none other than the mighty nation of the Philistines.

Footnotes

63:1 . . . The town of . . . over the land Beth-Omri . . . I cast its whole extent under the rule of Assyria: I put my officials as lieutenants over it. Ḥanunu of Gaza fled before my arms, and escaped to Egypt. Gaza I plundered, its possessions and its gods . . . and I put my royal image (?)—in his palace. I laid the service of the gods of his land under the service of Asshur. I laid tribute upon him . . . As a bird he flew hither (made submission) and I set him again to his place.'—*Keilinschriftliche Bibliothek*, ii, pp. 32, 33; Schrader, *Keilinschriften*³, p. 56. See also Rost, *Keilinschr. Tiglath-Pilesers*, p. 78.

64:1 'Azuri, king of Ashdod, devised in his heart to bring no more tribute, and sent an invitation to the kings of his neighbourhood to hostility against Asshur. On account of the misdeeds he wrought, I removed him from the lordship of the people of his land and put his brother Aḥimiti in lordship over them. But evil-plotting Hittites were hostile to his lordship and set over themselves Yamani, who had no claim to the throne, who like them had no respect for my lordship. In my fury I did not send the whole body of my troops. . . . I led merely the body-guard, who follows me wherever I go, to Ashdod. But Yamani fled as I approached to the border of Egypt, which lies beside Meluḫḫa, and was seen no more. I besieged and plundered Ashdod, Gath, and Ashdodimmu ["The port of Ashdod," מיה אשדוד or, "Gath of the Ashdodites," according to some interpreters], and carried off as booty their goods, women, sons and daughters, property, the palace treasures, and the people of the land. I re-peopled those towns anew . . . and put my lieutenants over them and counted them to the people of Assyria.'—*Keil. Bibl.* ii, pp. 66, 67. *KAT*³. p. 71.

65:1 Menahem of the town of Samaria, Ethba'al of Sidon, Mitinti of Ashdod [and a number of others] all the kings of the West brought rich presents . . . and kissed my feet. And Zidḳa, the king of Ashkelon, who had not submitted to my yoke, the gods of his house, himself, his wife, his sons, his daughters, his brothers, the seed of his house, I dragged off and brought them to Assyria. Sarludari, the son of Rukipti, their former king, I set again as king over the people of Ashkelon, took tribute and submission from him, and he became obedient to me. In the course of my expedition, I besieged Beth-Dagon, Joppa, Bene-Barka, Azuri, the towns of Zidḳa, which had not promptly submitted to me: I plundered them and dragged booty away from them. The principal men of Amḳarruna (Ekron) who had cast Padi, who by the right and oath of Assyria was the king, into fetters and delivered him up to Hezekiah of Judah, who had shut him in prison—their heart feared. The kings of the land of Egypt sent archers, chariots, and horses of the king of Meluḫḫa, a countless army, and came to help them. Their army stood against me before the town El-Tekeh, they raised their weapons. Trusting in Asshur, my Lord, I fought with them and subdued them; I took the chiefs of the chariots and the son of one of the kings of Egypt, and the chief of the chariots of the king of Meluḫḫa prisoners with my own hand in the *mêlée:* I besieged El-Tekeh and Timnath, and plundered them and took away their booty. Then I turned before Ekron, the chief men who had done evil I slew and hung their bodies on poles round the city: the inhabitants who had done evil I led out as prisoners: with the rest, who had done no evil, I made peace. Padi their king I led from Jerusalem and put him again on the throne of his lordship. I laid the tribute of my lordship upon him. Of Hezekiah . . . I besieged forty-six fortified towns . . . his towns which I had plundered, I took from his land and gave them to Mitinti, king of Ashdod, Padi, king of Ekron, and Zilbel, king of Gaza, and I cut his land short. To the former tribute I added the tribute due to my lordship and laid it upon them.'—*KB.* ii, pp. 90–95.

65:2 KB. ii, pp. 148, 149, and 238–241.

66:1 See Meyer's *History of the City of Gaza*, p. 38. Noordtzij, *De Filistijnen*, p. 171, identifies it with Kadesh, which is reasonable.

66:2 Neb. iv. 7. See also Ps. lxxxiii, which, according to the most likely view, was composed during the anxieties attending the restoration of Jerusalem.

CHAPTER III. THE LAND OF THE PHILISTINES

THE country of the Philistines is definitely limited, in Joshua xiii. 2, between the Shīḫōr or 'River of Egypt', the present Wady el-Arīsh, on the Egyptian frontier, which joins the sea at Rhinocolura—and 'the borders of Ekron northward, which is counted to the Canaanites'. Westward it was bounded by the Mediterranean Sea: eastward by the foothills of the Judean mountains. From Deuteronomy ii. 23 we learn that this territory had previously been in the possession of a tribe called *'Avvim*, of whom we know nothing but the name: from the passage in Joshua just quoted it would appear that a remnant of these aborigines still remained crowded down to the south. They may possibly have been of the same stock as the neolithic pre-Semitic people whose remains were found at Gezer. No doubt, as in the majority of cases of the kind, they survived as a substratum of the population in the rest of their ancient territory as well, engaged in the hard manual labour to which the wily Gibeonites were condemned.

We also learn from Joshua (xi. 21) that there was a Rephaite or 'Anakim' remnant left in some of the chief cities of the Philistine territory, which must have been of considerable importance, to judge from the stories of giant champions analysed on a previous page. How far the alliance of these formidable aborigines (which probably represent a pre-Canaanite immigration, later than the insignificant *'Avvim*) enabled the southern Philistines to hold their ground so much longer than the northern Zakkala is an interesting question the answer to which, however, could be nothing more than speculative.

Though no ancient authority definitely states it, there can hardly be any doubt that the repulse of the great attack on Egypt, in the days of Ramessu III, was the event which led to the permanent settlement of the Cretan tribes on the coastland. It is possible, indeed, that they already occupied the country as a military base for their operations against Egypt: the description, in the Medinet Habu temple, of the advance of the invaders through the lands of the Hittites and North Syrians makes this at least not improbable. However the exact details of chronology work out, we cannot dissociate the invasion of Egypt from the contemporaneous settlement by foreigners on the sea-coast.

Israel was already, as we learn from the stela of Merneptah, established in the promised land; and the Hebrew tribes had already been reinforced by the contingent of Egyptian serfs (possibly the enslaved descendants of the Bedawin invaders known to history as the Hyksos) and Kenites, whose traditions became the received version of Hebrew *origines*. The tribe of Dan, situated on the seacoast, was driven inland, and forced to establish itself elsewhere: but as we have seen, the whole length of the shore was occupied by the intruders, even north of Joppa. Wen-Amon has chronicled for us the settlement of Zakkala at Dor: that Sisera belonged to this tribe is also highly probable: and the remarkable developments displayed by the Phoenicians which distinguished them from all other Semites—developments to be noted in the following chapter—make it no longer possible to doubt that a very large Philistine or Zakkala element entered into the composition of that people.

In the earlier part of the history, as we have already indicated, the empire of the Philistines was widely spread over the country. As is well known, the name *Palestine* is merely a corruption of *Philistia;* and when Zephaniah or one of his editors calls Canaan 'the land of the Philistines' (ii. 4) he is expressing little more than what was at one time a fact. Their domination over the Hebrews is insisted on in both Judges and Samuel: the early kings of the Hebrews are elected with the specific purpose of freeing the people frown the foreign yoke: a governor is established in a town close to Jerusalem: even at Beth-Shan, at the inner end of the plain

Esdraelon, which once swarmed with the chariots of Sisera, the Philistines were able to fix Saul's body as a trophy: and the course of the history shows that they were there established in sufficient strength and with sufficient permanence to make the recovery of the trophy difficult.

The name of Beth-Dagon, the house of their chief god, is found among the towns enumerated to the northern coast-dwellers of the tribe of Asher (Joshua xix. 27); and there was a similarly named and better known town in the land of the southern Philistines; but these names, as we shall see in the following chapter, are older than the Philistine settlement. 'The stronghold above Jericho called Dagon

(mentioned in Josephus, *Ant.* xiii. 8. 1, *Wars*, i. 2. 3) is no doubt the same as Dok (now 'Ain ed-Dūk) where Simon was murdered (1 Macc. xvi. 15): probably the form of the name in Josephus is an error. There is a modern Beit Dejan near Nablus, which marks a third place of the same name, not recorded in history.

The Northern tribe of the foreigners must have become early absorbed by their Semitic neighbours. The Southern people, however, seated on their rich coast-plain and established in their powerful metropolitan cities, were longer able to maintain their ethnic independence. The wars of David drove them back on the coast, and reduced them to a subordinate position; and, as the names of the kings recorded in the Assyrian records show, they rapidly became semitized as time went on. As we have seen in the last chapter, however, their national traditions fought a long fight against absorption and oblivion. The pride of the Philistines—their persistent refusal to submit to Hebrew prejudices, such as the tabu against eating flesh with the blood and forbidden meats—was as offensive to Deutero-Zechariah (ix. 7) as is the pride of the Irish or Welsh nationalist to the average Englishman. Though in the later history we hear so little about them, they must still have been troublesome neighbours; otherwise there would not be such a constant chain of prophetic denunciations. Amos first, then Isaiah, Zephaniah, Joel, and the later prophets Jeremiah, Ezekiel, and Zechariah all pronounce woes upon them. One of Ezekiel's strongest denunciations of the corruptions of his own people well expresses the national hatred—even the daughters of the Philistines are ashamed at contemplating them (Ezek. xvi. 27). The son of Sirach says that 'his heart abhorreth them that sit upon the mountains of Samaria, and them that dwelt among the Philistines' (Ecclus. l. 26). Except for the naturalized Philistines in David's entourage, there is but one lull in the storm of war between the two nations throughout the Old Testament. This is in the charming poem, Psalm lxxxvii, written apparently under some one of the later kings. The psalmist pictures Yahweh enthroned upon His best-loved seat, the holy mountains of Zion, and reading, as it were, a census-roll of His people. This one was born in Egypt or Babylon—that one in Philistia or Tyre—yet all own Zion as their common Mother. The psalm is a miniature edition of the Book of Jonah: the poet's large-hearted universalism looks forward to an abolition of national jealousies.

Their cities all existed from pre-Philistine days. They are all, except the Beth-Dagons, mentioned in the Tell el-Amarna correspondence, and were then already communities of importance: how much farther back their history may go it is impossible to tell. Like the Hebrews, who appear to have added only one city—Samaria—to those which they inherited in the Promised Land, the Philistines were not city builders. Indeed we hardly would expect this of the 'Peoples of the Sea'. Ziklag, somewhere in the south of the Philistine territory, but not yet identified satisfactorily, may have been a new foundation: this, however, rests merely upon the vague circumstance that it has been impossible to find a satisfactory Semitic etymology for the name, which conceivably echoes the name of the Zakkala. If so, we understand better how the *southern* sept of the Philistines comes to be specifically called 'Cherethites'. or 'Cretans'. On the other hand, we elsewhere find the Zakkala in the *north*.

The five metropolitan cities of the Philistines were Gaza, Ashkelon, Gath, Ashdod, and Ekron. The first-mentioned is the only one of the five that still retains anything of its former importance. It is a modern, well-watered, and populous town, standing on the ancient site, and in the form *Ghuzzeh* retaining the ancient name. It is prominent in the Samson epic. We have already noticed the revolt of its leader, Hanunu, against the king of Assyria—a revolt that led to the battle of Raphia (710 B.C.), the first struggle between Egypt and Assyria. From Amos i. 6 we learn that Gaza was the centre of a slave-trade, which added bitterness to the relations between the Philistines and their Israelite neighbours. In 332 B.C. the city was besieged for two months by Alexander the Great. Its later history but slightly concerns us, though we may mention its total destruction by Alexander Jannaeus. It recovered even from this catastrophe, and we find it in the second and third centuries A. D. as the centre of worship of a deity peculiar to itself, called *Marna*, the ritual of whose service recalls in some respects that of the rites of Dagon. This cult, indeed, was probably the last relic of the Philistines, apart from the vague modern traditions to which we have already referred.

The city was surrounded by a wall, and watch-towers were erected at a distance from it, to give warning as early as possible of the approach of an enemy (2 Kings xviii. 8). 1 A neighbouring harbour town, called Μαιουμᾶ Γάζης, was of considerable importance and for a time was the site of a bishopric.

Ashkelon was the only city of the five that stood on the seacoast, though other maritime cities, such as Joppa, were (at least from time to time) also in Philistine hands. Its harbour, though inadequate for modern use, was sufficient for the small ships of antiquity. Samson visited Ashkelon to seize the wager he was obliged to pay after his riddle had been solved. 2 It is, however, from much later times—Maccabean, early Arab, and Crusader—that the chief historical importance of the city dates. These lie outside our present scope. We need not do more than mention the etymological speculations of Stephanus of Byzantium, who tells us that this city was founded by Askalos, brother of Tantalos and son of Hymenaios; and the statement of Benjamin of Tudela that Ezra re-founded Ashkelon under the name Benebrah. 1

Gath, reasonably identified with the enormous mound known as Tell eṣ-Ṣāfi at the embouchure of the Valley of Elah, had a different history from the rest. It seems in the time of the greatest extension of the Philistine power to have been the principal city of the five: at least the application to its ruler Achish of the title *melek*, 'king' (rather than the technical term *ṣeren*, applied normally to the 'lords' of the Philistines), if not a mere inadvertence, suggests that at least he was *primus inter pares*. He has, however, to bow to the wishes of his colleagues in the matter of David's alliance with him. In David's lament over Saul and Jonathan, Gath and Ashkelon are the two prominent cities specially mentioned; and (probably through the influence of that popular lay) 'tell it not in Gath' became a current catchword, which we meet once again in Micah i. 10. It is not infrequently used as such among ourselves; but in Hebrew it has a further aid to popularity in an alliteration, as though one should say 'gad not in Gath'.

But as we have already noticed, the name drops out from all references to the Philistines in the later literature: the Pentapolis becomes a Tetrapolis, and the hegemony passes over to Ashdod, which in time becomes the last typical Philistine city. This cannot be explained, however, by a total destruction of the city of Gath. For the excavations carried on by the Palestine Exploration Fund in 1900 at Tell eṣ-Ṣāfi showed that the site had been continuously occupied from very early times to the days of a modern village, whose houses and extensive graveyards seal up the secrets of the greater part of this important mound from the curiosity of the explorer. The true explanation is, that from the time of its conquest by Uzziah, Gath was reckoned a city of Judah by the Hebrew prophets. In the gradual shrinking of the Philistine border it would be one of the first to fall into Hebrew hands.

A destruction of Gath—probably the sacking by Uzziah—was still fresh in memory when Amos prophesied, and was used by hint as an illustration to enforce his denunciation of Samaria (vi. 2); in his first chapter we already find Gath omitted from the list of Philistine cities; and the reference immediately afterwards to 'the remnant of the Philistines' (i. 8) suggests that that people had shortly before suffered loss. In iii. 9 the words 'publish in the palaces at Ashdod' may possibly be an adaptation of the proverbial catchword already mentioned, modified to suit the altered circumstances. It likewise is assonantal in Hebrew.

Sargon, it is true, shortly after Uzziah's time, calls the city 'Gath of the Ashdodites' (if this be the correct translation of the phrase); but no doubt it was a matter of indifference in the eyes of the great king which of two trumpery communities claimed the possession of a town, so long as he himself had a satisfying share of the plunder.

It is unfortunate that the city had such a commonplace name. Its meaning, 'winepress,' was applicable to many sites, and it was evidently used for snore places than one. This makes the reconstruction of the history of Gath rather difficult. Thus, the Gath fortified by Rehoboam (2 Chron. xi. 8) can hardly be the Philistine city of that name; and certain other places such as Gath-hepher, Gath-rimmon, and Moresheth-gath, must be carefully distinguished therefrom. The same word appears in the *Gethsemane* of the New Testament.

Ashdod, the city to which the ark was first taken, is now represented by an insignificant village, whose only object of interest is the ruin of a large Saracenic *khan:* but ruins of more important buildings seem to have been seen here by seventeenth-century travellers. 1 Yet it must have been a city of special importance in the Pentapolis. Like Gaza, it had its 'palaces' (Amos iii. 9). As we have seen, Ashdod longest preserved the Philistine national tradition. 'The speech of Ashdod' lasted down to the time of Nehemiah. The temple of Dagon stood there till destroyed by the Maccabees (1 Macc. x. 83, 84). But the 'altars and gods' of the city, destroyed by Judas a few years before (1 Macc. v. 68), were perhaps objects rather of *Hellenic* cult, which at this date was well established in Western Palestine.

The great siege of Ashdod by Psammeticus, already referred to, is unknown to us except from Herodotus. It seems almost incredibly protracted, and probably there is something wrong with Herodotus' figures. Jeremiah's references to the *remnant* of Ashdod (xxv. 20) and Zephaniah's emphasis on a siege which shall drive out Ashdod at the noonday (ii. 4)—i.e. which shall last half a day only—are plausibly supposed to imply allusion to this event. A small inlet in the neighbouring coastline served Ashdod for a harbour: it is now called *Mīnet el-Ḳalʻah*, 'the harbour of the fortress': a tradition of some fortification of the harbour is thus preserved, as well as the Greek name λίμνη which has been transformed into the Arabic El-Mīneh; the initial λ having been mistaken for the Arabic article.

Ekron, since the time of Robinson, has always been equated to the village of 'Akir, now the site of a flourishing Jewish colony, whose red roofs are conspicuous on the seaward side of the Jerusalem railway soon after leaving Ramleh. But there are no remains of any ancient occupation here commensurate with the importance of the place. 'There are a few local traditions in 'Akir, but they are quite vague. Bauer (*Mittheilungen d. deutsch. Pal. Vereins*, 1899, p. 43) describes a visit he paid to the old mosque, the one stone building in the fellah village, erected on its highest point. There is a forecourt and portico with two rows of pillars. The thresholds are of marble. An old sheikh told him that the mosque was as old as the time of Abraham; but many such tales are told in Palestine of comparatively modern buildings. Ekron, if the place of the ancient oracle of Baal-zebub were really at 'Akir, has vanished utterly, leaving scarcely a potsherd behind. This is not what usually happens to ancient Palestine cities. With some hesitation I venture on the following suggestions.

To me there seems to be a confusion between two places of the same name. In Joshua xiii. 1–3, where the land not possessed by Joshua is detailed, we find mention made of the region of the Philistines and of the little southern tribe of the Geshurites, to 'the border of Ekron-Ṣaphōnah, *which is counted to the Canaanites*', and also the five lords of the *Philistines*, among which by contrast are enumerated the Ekronites. This expression 'Ekron-Ṣaphōnah' is correctly translated 'Ekron northward' in the English Bible; but it can also mean 'Northern Ekron', which to me seems here to give a more intelligible sense.

Again, in Joshua xv. 11 we find the border of the territory of Judah as running 'unto the side of Ekron-Ṣaphōnah'; an expression which I take to mean that this city, though adjoining the territory of Judah, was actually beyond its border. If so, it would be in the tribe of Dan; and in Joshua xix. 43 we actually find an Ekron enumerated among the Danite towns. Here, as there is no ambiguity, the qualifying adjective 'Northern' is omitted. The Southern Ekron would then belong to the tribe of Judah, in the theoretical scheme elaborated in the book of Joshua; and we find it duly mentioned, between Mareshah and Ashdod.

Again, the story of the rout after the battle of Ephes-Daminim (1 Sam. xvii. 52–54) is suggestive. The pursuit went 'by the way to the two gates, to Gath and to Ekron'. 'Akir, the usual site given for Ekron, cannot be spoken of a gate, in the sense that Gath, commanding as it does the mouth of the valley of Elah, can be so termed; and a chase of the Philistines prolonged *through Philistine territory* for such a long distance as from Gath to 'Akir is not very probable. We seem to find the other gate at a subsidiary outlet of the Valley of Elah, to the south of Gath, where stands a village called Dhikerīn. And Dhikerīn lies exactly in a straight line between Beit Jibrīn and 'Esdūd, the modern representatives of Mareshah and Ashdod.

Written in English letters, 'Dhikerīn' is not unlike 'Ekron' in general appearance. But philologically there can be no direct connexion between them, and my arguments in favour of the identification here suggested rest on grounds different from the superficial similarity of name. The single letter *k* in English represents two entirely different sounds in Hebrew and Arabic; one of these (כ) appears in '*Dhikerin*', the other (ק) in *Ekron*, as in *'Akir*. These letters can be treated as interchangeable in one case only. As in English, so in Greek, one sound and one character represent these two letters: and if for a while a district had become thoroughly Hellenized, the Greek κ might have been (so to speak) as a 'bridge' for the passing of one sound into the other. When the Semitic speech reasserted itself, it might have taken up the name with the wrong *k*. There is thus a possibility that a different word has become substituted for a half-forgotten and wholly misunderstood Hebrew name. But no stress can be laid upon this possible accident.

Dhikerin presents obvious signs of antiquity. Great artificial caves and huge cisterns are cut in the rock, testifying to its former importance, and it has never been finally identified with any other ancient site, though some of the earlier explorers have thought to find here no less a place than Gath itself. The Talmuds have nothing to say about it save that the name is derived from ארכד 'male', because the women there all bear male children. 1 Clermont-Ganneau (*Recueil d'arch. orient.* iv. 254) suggests a connexion between this place-name and that of the Zakkala.

Let us now look back for a moment to the story of the wanderings of the Ark. Suppose that the Gittites, when the plague broke out among them, sent the Ark, not to 'Akin, but to Dhikerin—which way much nearer and more convenient—we have then an immediate answer to an obvious difficulty. Why did the Philistines expect the ark to go anywhere near Beth-Shemesh at all? We must remember that they were not merely trying to get rid of the ark: they were on the look-out for a sign that the pestilence was a manifestation of the wrath of the God of the Hebrews. They must therefore have expected the Ark to return whence it had come, to the sanctuary at Shiloh, of whose existence and importance they could not have been ignorant. This was the natural goal of the sacred symbol, north of the great Canaanite wedge that centred in Jerusalem and separated the northern Israelites from their brethren in the south. From Shiloh the Ark had been taken: Shiloh was the chief centre of Hebrew religious life at the time: and to Shiloh the Ark should be expected to find its way back. [1] Therefore, if it was at the time in 'Akir, it ought to have gone by the northern valley route, into the Valley of Aijalon, so striking into the road for Shiloh some ten miles north of Jerusalem. If from 'Akir it went southward it would be shunted off south of the Canaanites into the southern territory, where no specially important shrine of the period is recorded. From 'Akir, therefore, it should not go within miles of Beth-Shemesh. But from Dhikerin, the only way toward Shiloh, avoiding Jerusalem, is by a valley route that leads straight to Beth-Shemesh and perforce passes that town.

Further evidence is given us by the story of the march of Sennacherib. That monarch was engaged in reducing places easily identified as the modern Jaffa, Yazur, Ibn Berak, and Beit Dejan, when the Ekrouites leagued themselves with the North Arabians and the Egyptians. Sennacherib met the allies at El-Tekeh, a place unfortunately not identified: it presumably was near the Northern Ekron, as the two places are mentioned together as border towns in Dan, Joshua xix. 40. This Northern Ekron, we may agree, might well be represented by 'Akir, whose poverty in antiquities accords with the apparent insignificance of the Danite town. Close to 'Akir is a village in the plain, called Zernukah, a name which may possibly echo the name of El-Tekeh. In any case Sennacherib was victorious and then went straight to Timnath, which he reduced, after which he proceeded to attack Ekron. This order of proceedings is inconsistent with 'Akir as the site of Ekron. Sennacherib's successful progress against the south we should expect to proceed steadily southward, involving an attack on 'Akir before the reduction of Timnath. Ekron must therefore have been south from Tibneh, which fits the conditions of the site now suggested.

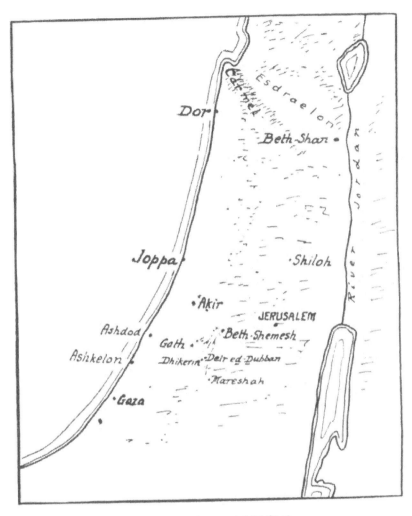

Fig 3. Sketch-map of Philistia.

The denunciations of Ekron in the prophetic books help us very little in the solution of the problem. But there is a suggestive hint in the opening verses of 2 Kings. Ahaziah having met with an accident sent to inquire of Baal-zebub 'lord of flies', the god of Ekron, as to his prospects of recovery. When we find that less than a couple of miles from Dhikerin there is a village bearing the name of *Deir edh-Dhubhān*, 'the convent of the flies', we feel some justification in asking, can it be that Baal-zebub still rules his ancient lordship?

The land of the Philistines, dominated by these five cities, has been so often described that it is needless to waste space in an account of it. Briefly, we may say that whoever held that part of the country was at an enormous advantage. With the possible exception of the plain of Esdraelon, it is the most fertile land in Western Palestine. Though there are few perennial streams, water can be found wherever one chooses to dig for it. Through it runs the great trade-route from Egypt by Damascus to Babylon. The mart of Gaza is the natural rendezvous of all who have commerce with Arabia. The seaports of Southern Palestine are all commanded, as are the valleys which are the doorways to the Hinterland: so that the coast dwellers can engage in commerce on their own account, while at the same time they can control the progress and civilization among the aliens in the interior. When we stand on some eminence that commands this rich strip of territory we find it easy to understand the bitterness with which through the centuries the Hebrews regarded the Philistines.

Footnotes

71:1 So a sentry-station was established on a hill some way S. of Gezer: see my *Excavation of Gezer*, vol. ii, p. 365.

71:2 It has been suggested that this took place not at Ashkelon, but at a small site p. 72 in the valley of Elah called *Khurbet* (= ruin) 'Aṣḳalân. This is certainly nearer to Timnath, but there are here no traceable remains older than the Roman period.

72:1 A description of the remains at Ashkelon, with a plan, will be found in the *Quarterly Statement* of the Palestine Exploration Fund for January 1913.

73:1 See Sepp, *Jerusalem and das heilige Land*, vol. ii, p. 598.

75:1 Neubauer, *Geog. d. Talm.* p. 71.

76:1 Meyer, *Gesch. d. Alterthums*, i, p. 358, suggests from Jer. vii. 14, that Shiloh was destroyed. But the space of time between Samuel and Jeremiah is so long, that many unrecorded events might have taken place in the meanwhile: and, indeed, Shiloh is still an important sanctuary in 1 Sam. xiv. 3.

CHAPTER IV. THE CULTURE OF THE PHILISTINES

I. Their Language.

OF the language of the Philistines we are profoundly ignorant. An inscription in their tongue, written in an intelligible script, would be one of the greatest rewards that an explorer of Palestine could look for. As yet, the only materials we have for a study of the Philistine language are a few proper names, and possibly some words, apparently non-Semitic, embedded here and there in the Hebrew of the Old Testament. Thus, our scanty information is entirely drawn from foreign sources. We are exactly in the same position as a student of some obscure Oriental language would be, if his only materials were the names of natives as reported in English newspapers. Now, we are all familiar with the barbarous and meaningless abbreviation 'Abdul', applied with various depreciatory epithets to a certain ex-potentate. Some time ago a friend called my attention to a paragraph in, I think, a Manchester paper, describing how a certain Arab 'named Sam Seddon' had been prosecuted for some offence: though the 'Arabian Nights' is almost an English classic, the reporter had failed to recognize the common name *Shems ed-Din*! If we were obliged to reconstruct the Arabic language from materials of this kind, we could hardly expect to get very far; but in attempting to recover something of the Philistine language we are no better off.

The one common noun which we know with tolerable certainty is *ṣeren*, the regular word in the Hebrew text for the 'lords' by which the Philistines were governed: a word very reasonably compared with the Greek τύραννος. 1 This, however, does not lead us very far. It happens that no satisfactory Indo-European etymology has been found for τύραννος, so that it may be a word altogether foreign to the Indo-European family. In any case, one word could hardly decide the relationship of the Philistine language any more than could 'benval' (*sic!*) decide the relationship of Pictish in the hands of Sir Walter Scott's amateur philologists.

The word *ṣeren* is once used (1 Kings vii. 30) as a technical term for some bronze objects, part of the 'bases' made for the temple (wheel-axles?). This is probably a different word with different etymological connexions. The word mᵉkōnah in the list cited below, is found in the same verse.

Renan, in his so-called *Histoire du peuple d'Israël*, has collected a list of words which he suggests may have been imported into Hebrew from Philistine sources. That there should be such borrowing is *a priori* not improbable: we have already shown that the leaders among Hebrew speakers must have understood the Philistine tongue down to the time of David at least. But Renan's list is far from convincing. It is as follows:

parbār or parvār, 'a suburb': compare *peribolus*.

mᵉkōnah, something with movable wheels: compare *machina*.

mᵉkhērah, 'a sword': compare μάχαιρα.

caphtōr, 'a crown, chaplet': compare *capital*.

pīlegesh, 'a concubine': compare *pellex*.

A further comparison of the name of Araunah the Jebusite, on whose threshing-floor the plague was stayed (and therefore 'the place in Jerusalem from which pestilential vapours arose'!), with the neuter plural form *Averna*, need hardly he taken seriously.

But since Renan wrote, the discovery of the inscription on the Black Stone of the Forum has shown us what Latin was like, as near as we can get to the date of the Philistines, and gives us a warning against attempts to interpret supposed Philistine words by comparison with Classical Latin. And, even if the above comparisons be sound, the borrowing, as Noordtzij 1 justly remarks, might as well have taken place the other way; as is known to have happened in several cases which he quotes.

There is a word כובע or קובע meaning a 'helmet', the etymology of which is uncertain. 2 It may possibly be a Philistine word: the random use of כ and ק suggests that they are attempts to represent a foreign initial guttural (cf. *ante*, p. 75). Both forms are used in 1 Samuel xvii, the one ('כ) to denote the helmet of the *foreigner* Goliath, the other ('ק) that of the Hebrew Saul. No stress can, however, be laid on this distinction. The form 'ק is used of the helmets of the *foreigners* named in Ezekiel xxiii. 24, while 'כ is used of those of Uzziah's *Hebrew* army, 2 Chronicles xxvi. 14.

Of the place-names mentioned in the Old Testament there is not one, with the possible exception of Ziklag, which can be referred to the Philistine language. All are either obviously Semitic, or in any case (being mentioned in the Tell el-Amarna letters) are older than the Philistine settlement. Hitzig has made ingenious attempts to explain some of them by various Indo-European words, but these are not successful.

The persons known to us are as follows:

(1) *Abimelech*, the king who had dealings with Abraham. A Semitic name.

(2) *Aḥuzzath*, Counsellor of No. (1): Semitic name.

(3) *Phicol*, General of No. (1). Not explained as Semitic: possibly a current Philistine name adopted by the narrator.

(4) *Badyra*, king of Dor, in Wen-Amon's report. Probably not Semitic.

(5) *Warati*, a merchant, mentioned by Wen-Amon.

(6) *Makamaru*, a merchant, mentioned by Wen-Amon.

(7) *Dagon*, chief god of the Philistines.

(8) *Delilah*, probably not Philistine. See *ante*, p. 45.

(9) *Sisera*, king of Harosheth. See *ante*, p. 41, and compare Beneṣasira on the tablet of Keftian names.

(10) *Achish* or *Ekosh*, 1 apparently the standard Philistine name, like 'John' among ourselves. It seems to reappear in the old Aegean home in the familiar form *Anchises*. It occurs twice in the tablet of Keftian names (*ante*, p. 10) and in the Assyrian tablets it appears in the form *Ikausu*. 2

(11) *Maoch*, father of Achish, king of Gath. Unexplained and probably Philistine.

(12) *Ittai*, David's faithful Gittite friend, perhaps Philistine.

(13) *Obed-Edom*, a Gittite who sheltered the Ark: a pure Semitic name.

(14) *Goliath*, a Rephaite, and therefore not Philistine.

(15) *Saph*, a Rephaite, and therefore not Philistine.

(16) *Zaggi*, a person signing as witness an Assyrian contract tablet of the middle of the seventh century B.C. found at Gezer. The name is not explained, and may be Philistine.

(17–26) The ten Philistine kings mentioned on the Assyrian tablets, who without exception bear Semitic names. *Sarludâri* is an Assyrian name, which may possibly have been adopted by its bearer as a compliment to his master.

This list is so meagre that it is scarcely worth discussing. It will be observed that at the outside not more than eight of these names can be considered native Philistine.

Down to about the time of Solomon the Philistines preserved their linguistic individuality. A basalt statuette of one Pet-auset was found somewhere in the Delta, 1 in which he is described as an interpreter [hieroglyphs] 'for Canaan *and* Philistia'. There would be no point in mentioning the two places if they had a common language. Ashdod, we have seen, preserved a patois down to the time of Nehemiah; but it is clear that the Philistines had become semitized by the time of the operations of the Assyrian kings. It is likely that the Rephaite element in the population was the leaven through which the Philistines became finally assimilated in language and other customs to the surrounding Semitic tribes, as soon as their supremacy had been destroyed by David's wars. The Rephaites, of course, were primarily a pre-Semitic people: but probably they had themselves already become thoroughly semitized by Amorite influence before the Philistines appeared on the scene.

We have, besides, a number of documents which, when they have been deciphered, may help us in reconstructing the 'speech of Ashdod'. The close relationship of the Etruscans to the Philistines suggests that the Etruscan inscriptions may some time be found to have a bearing on the problem. It is also not inconceivable that some of the obscure languages of Asia Minor, specimens of which are preserved for us in the Hittite, Mitannian, Lycian, and Carian inscriptions may have light to contribute. The inscriptions of Crete, in the various Minoan scripts, and the Eteocretan inscriptions of Praesos 2 may also prove of importance in the investigation. Two other alleged fragments of the 'Keftian' language are at our service: the list of names already quoted on p. 10, which suggestively contains *Akašou* and *Beneṣasira*: and a magical formula in a medical MS. of the time of Thutmose III, published by Birch in 1871, 3 which contains *inter alia* the following—copied here from a corrected version published by Ebers. 1

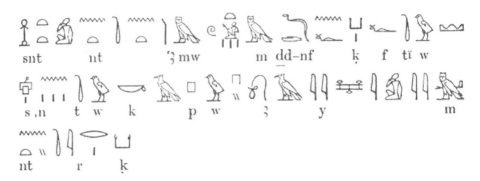

'Conjuration in the *Amu* language which people call Keftiu—*senutiukapuwaimantirek*' or something similar. This is not more intelligible than such formulae usually are. Mr. Alton calls my attention to the tempting resemblance of the last letters to trke, turke, θrke, a verb (?) common in the Etruscan inscriptions.

There is one document of conspicuous importance for our present purpose, although it is as yet impossible to read it. This is the famous disk of terra-cotta found in the excavation of the Cretan palace of Phaestos, and dated to the period known as Middle Minoan III—that is to say, about 1600 B.C. It is a roughly circular tablet of terra cotta, 15.8–16.5 cm. in diameter. On each face is a spiral band of four coils, indicated by a roughly drawn meandering line; and an inscription, in some form of picture-writing, has been impressed on this band, one by one, from dies, probably resembling those used by bookbinders. I suppose it is the oldest example of printing with movable types in the world. On one face of the disk, which I call Face I, there are 119 signs; on the other face, here called Face II, there are 123. They are divided into what appear to be word-groups, 30 in number on Face I and 31 on Face II, by lines cutting across the spiral bands at right angles. These word-groups contain from two to seven characters each. There are forty-five different characters employed. It is likely, therefore, from the largeness of this number that we have to deal with a *syllabary* rather than an alphabet.

I have discussed this inscription in a paper contributed to the *Proceedings* of the Royal Irish Academy, [2] to which I must refer the reader for the full investigation. Its special importance for our present purpose is based upon the fact that the most frequently used character, a man's head with a plumed head-dress, has from the moment of its first discovery been recognized as identical in type with the plumed head-dresses of the Philistine captives pictured at Medinet Habu. This character appears *only at the beginnings of words*, from which I infer that it is not a phonetic sign, but a determinative, most probably denoting personal names. Assuming this, it next appears that Face II consists of a list of personal names. Representing

Fig. 4 A. The Phaestos Disk (Face I).

each character by a letter, which is to be regarded as a mere algebraic symbol and not a phonetic sign, we may write the inscription on the disk in this form:

Face I (Fig. 4 A).

Mξχsh sβhw Muζc̱ χηs lδgξ ρζσi̱ taxl μhtaσ
χuϝη hδsw Mqvs sηya nδδgw ρzσ nla dwjxl Mπsa
nvhf nft ṉβh χnvhf smζη hσw hβh hζσδ χnvhf
πoxσh Mdwζh nmζη βh

Fig. 4 B. The Phaestos Disk (Face II).

Face II (Fig. 4 B): written as a list of names.
1. Mξtaσ δsξ nβh nnm
2. Mξbsl̄ sβhξ sϕf
3. Mξdσ(ϕ) kqw
4. Mξrrw arsh
5. Mξjζy xκ Ms$\eta\lambda\zeta\sigma$ pā Mξkq̄

6. Μξsswuθ lξ Μξkq Msηλζσ p̱a̱ Μξkq
7. Μξszjσs dσφτ̱ kqξ
8. Μξta ζτw λey
9. Μξsswuθ ta λey

There is just one type of ancient document which shows such a 'sediment', so to speak, of proper names at the end. This is a contract tablet, which ends with a list of witnesses, and in the paper above referred to I have put forward the conjecture that the disk is of this nature. In Face I, although not one word of the inscription can be deciphered, it will be found that, applying the clue of the proper names, everything fits exactly in its place, assuming the ordinary formula of a contract such as we find it in cuneiform documents.

The first two words would give us the name and title of the presiding magistrate: then comes the name of one of the contracting parties, uζc χηs: then come six words or word-groups, quite unintelligible, but not improbably stating what this person undertakes to do: then follows what would be the name of the other contracting party.

Next come some words which ought to give some such essential detail as the *date* of the contract. And we find among these words just what we want, a proper name πsa, denoting the officer who was eponymous of the year.

The last thirteen words we might expect to be a detailed inventory of the transaction, whatever its nature may have been. It is therefore satisfactory to notice that they arrange themselves neatly, just as they stand, in three parallel columns, having obvious mutual relations: thus—

nvhf	. . .	n-ft	n-βh	
χ-nvhf	s-mζη	h-sw	h-βh	h-ζσδ
χ-nvhf πoxσh Mdwζh	n-mζη		βh	

which table not only confirms the conclusions arrived at, but illustrates a rule that may also be inferred from the list of witnesses on Face II. Words are declined by prefixes ξ, s, n, h, χ and suffixes w, ξ; and *words in apposition have the same prefix*. See the third column of the above table, and the titles of witnesses 1, 2. We have a word βh in several forms: s-βh-w, n-β̱ẖ, h-β̱ẖ, s-βh-ξ. Further, ξ, prefixed to the 'name of the magistrate' and all the names of witnesses, probably means 'before, in the presence of'. The name which follows that of the two witnesses 5 and 6 is probably that of their father, and this assumed it follows that the prefix s probably has a genitive sense.

There remains one important point. At the bottom of certain characters there is a sloping line running to the left. This is always at the end of a word-group: the two apparent exceptions shown in some drawings of the disk (in word-groups 6 and 23 on Face II) being seemingly cracks in the surface of the disk. The letters marked are underlined in the transcript given above. I suggest with regard to these marks that they are meant to express a modification of the phonetic value of the character, too slight to require a different letter to express it, but too marked to allow it to be neglected altogether. And obviously the most likely modification of the kind would be the elision of the vowel of a final open syllable. The mark would thus be exactly like the *virāma* of the Devanāgarī alphabet. [1] When we examine the text, we find that it is only in certain words that this mark occurs. It is found in βh, however declined, except when the suffixes w, ξ are present. It is found in the word nvhf, however declined, and appears in the two similar words μhtaσ and Mξtaσ. It is found in the personal name kq (in the formula pa Mξkq). There are only one or two of the eighteen examples of its use outside these groups, and probably if we had some more examples of the script, or a longer text, these would be found to fit likewise into series. This stroke would therefore be a device to express a final closed syllable. Thus, if it was desired to write the name of the god *Dagon*, it would be written on this theory, let us say, DA-GO-NA, with a stroke underneath the last symbol to elide its vowel. The consequences that may follow if this assumption should at any time be proved, and the culture which the objects represented by the various signs indicate, are subjects for discussion in later sections of this chapter. For further details of the analysis of the disk I must refer to my *Royal Irish Academy* paper above quoted: I have dwelt on it here, because if, as is most probable, the plumed head-dress shows that in this disk we have to deal with 'proto-Philistines', we must look to this document and others of the same kind, with which excavators of the future may be rewarded, to tell us something of the language of the people with whom we have to deal.

Footnotes

79:1 The 'Lords of the Philistines' are, however, in the Greek Version called σατράπαι; but in Judges (except iii. 3), Codex Vaticanus and allied MSS. have ἄρχοντες, a rendering also found sometimes in Josephus.

80:1 *De Filistijnen*, p. 81.

80:2 Cf. Latin *cappa*, &c. (?).

81:1 Max Müller in his account of the school-tablet (ante, p. 10) compares the Assyrian form Ikausu and the Greek Ἀγχοῦς, and infers that the true pronunciation of the name was something like *Ekôsh*.

81:2 But in the last edition of *KAT*. p. 437, it is noticed that this name can possibly be read Ikasamsu or Ikasamsu.

82:1 See the description by Chassinat, *Bulletin de l'inst. franç. d'arch. au Caire*, i. (1901), p. 98.

82:2 See Conway in the *Annual of the British School at Athens*, vol. viii, p. 125, for an exhaustive analysis of these inscriptions.

82:3 *Zeitschr. f. ägypt. Sprache* (1871), p. 61.

83:1 *Zeitschr. der D. M. G.* xxxi, pp. 451, 452.

83:2 *Proceedings of the Royal Irish Academy*, vol. xxx, section C, p. 342.

87:1 I find that this comparison has been anticipated in an article in Harper's Magazine (European Edition, vol. lxi, p. 187), which I have read since writing the above. The rest of the article, I regret to say, does not convince me.

II. THEIR ORGANIZATION.

A. *Political.*

From the time when the Philistines first appear in their Palestinian territory they are governed by *Lords*, ṣerānīm, each of whom has domination in one of the five chief cities, but who act in council together for the common good of the nation. They seem, indeed, to engage personally in duties which an Oriental monarch would certainly delegate to a messenger. They negotiate with Delilah. They convene the great triumph-feast to which Samson put so disastrous an end. There is a democratic instinct manifested by the men of Ashdod and Ekron, who peremptorily 'summoned' the council of lords to advise them what to do on the outbreak of plague: just as the merchants of the Zakkala obliged even a forceful ruler like Zakar-Baal to make an unsatisfactory compromise in the matter of Wen-Amon, and in much later times the people of Ekron deposed and imprisoned a ruler who persisted in the unpopular course of submission to Assyria. Achish makes arrangements with David, which his colleagues overrule. Of the methods of election of these officers we know absolutely nothing. From the Assyrian documents we hear of a series of rulers over Ashdod, father and son, but this does not necessarily prove that the hereditary principle was recognized. Such a political organization was quite unlike that of the nations round about: but the government of the Etruscans, who, as we have seen, were probably a related race, presents some analogy. There is a considerable similarity between the *lucumones* of Etruria and the Philistine ṣerānīm.

Nowhere do we read of a king of the Philistines. ₁ To infer, as has actually been done, from 1 Kings iv. 21 ('Solomon ruled over all the kingdoms from the River unto the land of the Philistines') that their territory was organized as a kingdom, displays a sad lack of a sense of humour. When Hebrew writers speak of 'a king of Gath' (1 Sam. xxvii. 2), 'him that holdeth the sceptre from Ashkelon' (Amos i. 8), 'all the kings of the land of the Philistines' (Jer. xxv. 20), 'the king [perishing] from Gaza' (Zech. ix. 5), they obviously are merely offering a Hebrew word or periphrasis as a translation of the native Philistine title. The same is true of the analogous expressions in the Assyrian tablets. The case of the Etruscan 'kings' seems exactly similar, though there appears to have been an Achish-like king in Clusium.

In Gibeah, and probably in other towns as well, a resident officer, like a Turkish *mudir*, was maintained at the time of their greatest power.

It is possible that, if we had before us all the documents relating to the history of the Philistines, we might be able to divide them into clans, corresponding perhaps in some degree to the threefold division of the Egyptian monuments—Zakkala, Washasha, and Pulasati, i.e. as we have tried to show already, Cretans, Rhodians, and Carians. The continually recurring phrase 'Cherethites and Pelethites' suggests some twofold division. Ezekiel xxv. 16 ('Behold, I will stretch out my hand upon the Philistines, and I will cut off the Cherethites') may or may not imply a similar division. The report of the young Egyptian (1 Sam. xxx. 14) implies that the name 'Cherethites', if it had a specific meaning apart from 'Philistines', denoted the dwellers in the extreme south of Philistine territory: and we have already made passing note of the occurrence of the name Ziklag, a possible echo of the Zakkala, in that part of the country. The almost accidental allusion to Carians in the history of the kings must not be overlooked. But our data are so slender that very little can be built upon them. All we can say is that the origin of the Philistines makes it improbable that they were a single undivided tribe, and that the scanty hints which the history affords render it still more unlikely.

Nor can we necessarily infer that the peculiar government by a council of the lords of five cities implies that they were divided into five tribes. For though there seems to have been an actual division of the territory into districts, each of them under the hegemony of one of these cities, the limits are rather indefinite; and to judge from the scanty materials at our disposal, seem to have varied from time to time. The recurrence of the phrase '[such a city] and the border thereof' ₁ seems to indicate a definite division of the country into provinces governed each by one of the cities; and this is confirmed by David's speech to Achish, ₂ 'Give me a place in one of the cities in the country (הדשה ערי באחת,) for why should thy servant dwell in the royal city (הכלממה בעיר) with thee?' A similar polity is traceable in Etruria.

Of the division of the minor cities of the Philistine territory among the Pentapolis—perhaps Pentarchy would be a more correct term to use—we know very little. In the time of David's exile Ziklag was under the control of the king of Gath. Sargon, according to one interpretation of his inscription, supposes Gath itself to belong to Ashdod. We may compare 'Gazara that bordereth on Azotus' (1 Macc. xiv. 34), though they are about sixteen miles apart, and each only just visible on the other's horizon. Rather curiously, Joppa and the neighbouring villages depended, according to Sennacherib, on *Ashkelon*.

Besides these towns we hear of certain unwalled villages (1 Sam. vi. 18) which are not specified by name.

B. Military.

Certain functionaries called sārīm meet us from time to time in the history (1 Sam. xviii. 30, xxix. 3, 9). It is the sārīm whose protest prevents David from joining in the battle of Gilboa. The word is, of course, a commonplace Semitic term, and is applied in Deborah's Song to the princes of Issachar, and by Zephaniah to those of Jerusalem. Among the Philistines the officials denoted by this word were no doubt military captains.

It is obvious throughout the whole history, from the days of the Medinet Habu sculptures onwards, that the military forces of the Philistines were well organized. In 1 Samuel xiii. 5 we read of 30,000 chariots and 6,000 horsemen, which, even if the numbers are not to be taken literally, indicates a considerable wealth in war equipment. Elsewhere (ib. xxix. 2) we hear of 'hundreds and thousands', which may indicate a system of division into centuries and regiments. Of their methods of fighting we have no certain information: Judges i. 19 emphasizes their corps of war-chariots: in the account of the battle of Gilboa the archers are specially alluded to. The Medinet Habu sculptures and the description of the equipment of the champions are analysed in the following section.

C. Domestic.

On the subject of family life among the Philistines nothing is known. The high-minded sense of propriety attributed to Abimelech in the patriarchal narratives has already been touched upon. Samson's relations with his Timnathite wife can hardly be made to bear undue stress: a Semitic marriage of the ṣadīḳa type is pictured by the storyteller. The wife remains in her father's house and is visited by her husband from time to time. Men and women apparently mingle freely in the temple of Dagon at Gaza. No further information is vouchsafed us.

Footnotes

88:1 1 Except Abimelech, Gen. xxvi. 1. *Exceptio probat regulam.*

89:1 See Judg. i. 18, 1 Sam. v. 6, 2 Kings xviii. 8.

89:2 1 Sam. xxvii. 5.

III. Their Religion.

Of the religion of the Philistines we know just enough to whet a curiosity that for the present seeks satisfaction in vain. The only hints given us in the Old Testament history are as follows:

(1) The closing scene of Samson's career took place in a temple of Dagon at Gaza, which must have been a large structure, as different as possible from the native High Places of Palestine.

(2) In this temple sacrifices were offered at festivals conducted by the 'Lords' of the Philistines (Judg. xvi. 23). It is not unreasonable to suppose that Samson was destined to be offered in sacrifice at the great feast of rejoicing there described. This was probably an annual festival, occurring at a fixed time of the year, and not a special celebration of the capture of Samson: because an interval of some months, during which Samson's shorn hair grew again, must have taken place between the two events. We are reminded of the Athenian Θαργήλια, with Samson in the rôle of the φαρμακός. Human sacrifices were offered in the temple of Marna at Gaza down to the fourth century A. D., as we learn from a passage presently to be quoted from Marcus the Deacon.

(3) There was also a temple of Dagon at Ashdod, which indicates that the deity was a universal god of the Philistines, not a local divinity like the innumerable Semitic Ba'alim. Here there were priests, and here a rite of 'leaping on (or rather stepping over) the threshold' was observed. A sculptured image of the god stood in this temple.

(4) There was somewhere a temple of Ashtaroth (Samuel) or of Dagon (Chronicles) where the trophies of Saul were suspended. It is not expressly said that this temple was in Beth-shan, to the wall of which the body of Saul was fastened.

(5) The Philistines were struck with terror when the Ark of Yahweh was brought among them. Therefore they believed in (a) the existence and (b) the extra-territorial jurisdiction of the Hebrew deity. This suggests a wider conception of the limitations of divine power than was current among the contemporary Semites.

(6) Small portable images (עצבים) were worn by the Philistines and carried as amulets into battle (2 Sam. v. 21). 'This practice lasted till quite late (2 Macc. xii. 40).

(7) News of a victory was brought to the image-houses, probably because they were places of public resort, where they could be proclaimed (1 Sam. xxxi. 9).

(8) At Ekron there was an oracle of Baal-zebub, consulted by the Israelite king Ahaziah (2 Kings i. 2).

Let us clear the ground by first disposing of the last-named deity. This one reference is the only mention of him in the Old Testament, and indeed he is not alluded to elsewhere in Jewish literature. He must, however, have had a very prominent position in old Palestinian life, as otherwise the use of the name in the Gospels to denote the 'Prince of the Devils' (Matt. xii. 24, &c.) would be inexplicable. A hint in Isaiah ii. 6 shows us that the Philistines, like the Etruscans, were proverbial for skill in soothsaying, and it is not unlikely that the shrine of Baal-zebub should have been the site of their principal oracle. If so, we can be sure that Ahaziah was not the only Israelite who consulted this deity on occasion, and it is easy to understand that post-exilic reformers would develop and propagate the secondary application of his name in order to break the tradition of such illegitimate practices. It is, however, obvious that the Philistines who worked the oracle of Baal-zebub simply entered into an old Canaanite inheritance. This is clear from the Semitic etymology of the name. When they took over the town of Ekron and made it one of their chief cities, they naturally took over what was probably the most profitable source of emolument that the town contained. The local divinity had already established his lordship over the flies when the Philistines came on the scene.

This was no contemptible or insignificant lordship. A man who has passed a summer and autumn among the house-flies, sand-flies, gnats, mosquitoes, and all the other winged pests of the Shephelah will not feel any necessity to emend the text so as to give the Baʻal of Ekron 'a lofty house' or 'the Planet Saturn' or anything else more worthy of divinity 1; or to subscribe to Winckler's arbitrary judgement: 'Natürlich nicht Fliegenbaʻal, sondern Baʻal von Zebub, worunter man sich eine Oertlichkeit in Ekron vorzustellen hat, etwa den Hügel auf dem der Tempel stand' (*Geschichte Israels*, p. 224). The Greek Version lends no countenance to such euhemerisms, for it simply reads τῷ Βάαλ μυῖαν. Josephus avoids the use of the word *Baʻal*, and says 'he sent to the Fly' (*Ant.* ix. 2. 1). The evidence of a form with final *l* is, however, sufficiently strong to be taken seriously. Although the vocalization is a difficulty, the old explanation seems to me the best, namely, that the by-form is a wilful perversion, designed to suggest *zebel*, 'dung.' The Muslim *argot* which turns ḳiyámah (*Anastasis* = the Church of the Holy Sepulchre) into ḳumámah (dung-heap) is a modern example of the same kind of bitter wit.

The Lord of Flies is hardly a fly-averter, like the Ζεὺς ἀπόμυιος of Pliny and other writers, with whom he is frequently compared. In fact, what evidence there is would rather indicate that the original conception was a god in the bodily form of the vermin, the notion of an averter being a later development: that, for instance, *Apollo Smintheus* has succeeded to a primitive mouse-god, who very likely gave oracles through the movements of mice. That Baal-zebub gave oracles by his flies is at least probable. A passage of Iamblichus (*apud* Photius, ed. Bekker, p. 75) referring to Babylonian divinations has often been quoted in this connexion; but I think that probably mice rather than flies are there in question. Lenormant (*La divination chez les Chaldéens*, p. 93) refers to an omen-tablet from which auguries are drawn from the behaviour or peculiarities of flies, but unfortunately the tablet in question is too broken to give any continuous sense. 2

A curious parallel may he cited from Scotland. In the account of the parish of Kirkmichael, Banffshire, is a description (*Statistical Account of Scotland*, vol. xii, p. 464) of the holy well of St. Michael, which was supposed to have healing properties:

'Many a patient have its waters restored to health and many more have attested the efficacies of their virtues. But as the presiding power is sometimes capricious and apt to desert his charge, it now [A. D. 1794] lies neglected, choked with weeds, unhonoured, and unfrequented. In better days it was not so; for the winged guardian, *under the semblance of a fly*, was never absent from his duty. If the sober matron wished to know the issue of her husband's ailment, or the love-sick nymph that of her languishing swain, they visited the well of St. Michael. Every movement of the sympathetic fly was regarded in silent awe; and as he appeared cheerful or dejected, the anxious votaries drew their presages; their breasts vibrated with correspondent emotions. Like the Dalai Lama of Thibet, or the King of Great Britain, whom a fiction of the English law supposes never to die, the guardian fly of the well of St. Michael was believed to be exempted from the laws of mortality. To the eye of ignorance he might sometimes appear dead, but, agreeably to the Druidic system, it was only a transmigration into a similar form, which made little alteration in the real identity.'

In a foot-note the writer of the foregoing account describes having heard an old man lamenting the neglect into which the well had fallen, and saying that if the infirmities of years permitted he would have cleared it out and 'as in the days of youth enjoyed the pleasure of seeing the guardian fly'. Let us suppose the old man to have been eighty years of age: this brings the practice of consulting the fly-oracle of Kirkmichael down to the twenties of the eighteenth century, and probably even later.

Leaving out Baal-zebub, therefore, we have a female deity, called *Ashtaroth* (Aštoreth) in the passage relating to the temple of Bethshan, and a male deity called *Dagon*, ascribed to the Philistines. We may incidentally recall what was said in the first chapter as to the possibility of the obscure name Beth-Car enshrining the name of an eponymous Carian deity: it seems at least as likely as the meaning of the name in Hebrew, 'house of a lamb.' Later we shall glance at the evidence which the Greek writers preserve as to the peculiar cults of the Philistine cities in post-Philistine times, which no doubt preserved reminiscences of the old worship. In the meanwhile let us concentrate our attention on the two deities named above.

I. ASHTORETH. At first sight we are tempted to suppose that the Philistines, who otherwise succeeded in preserving their originality, had from the first completely succumbed to Semitic influences in the province of religion. 'As immigrants', says Winckler in his *Geschichte Israels*, 'they naturally adopted the civilization of the land they seized, and with it the cultus also.' And certainly Ashtaroth or Ashtoreth was *par excellence* the characteristic Semitic deity, and worshippers of this goddess might well be said to have become completely semitized.

But there is evidence that makes it doubtful whether the assimilation had been more than partial. We begin by noting that Herodotus 1 specially mentions the temple of ἡ Οὐρανία Ἀφροδίτη as standing at Ashkelon, and he tells us that it was the oldest of all the temples dedicated to this divinity, older even than that in Cyprus, as the Cyprians themselves admitted: also that the Scythians plundered the temple and were in consequence afflicted by the goddess with a hereditary νοῦσος θήλεια. 2 The remarkable inscription found at Delos, in which one Damon of Ashkelon dedicates an altar to his tutelary divinities, brilliantly confirms the statement of Herodotus. It runs:

ΔΙΙ ΟΥΡΙѠΙ ΚΑΙ ΑϹΤΑΡΤΗΙ ΠΑΛΑΙϹΤΙΝΗΙ

ΚΑΙ ΑΦΡΟΔΙΤΗΙ ΟΥΡΑΝΙΑΙ ΘΕΟΙϹ ΕΠΗΚΟΟΙϹ

ΔΑΜѠΝ ΔΗΜΗΤΡΙΟΥ ΑϹΚΑΛѠΝΙΤΗϹ

ϹѠΘΕΙϹ ΑΠΟ ΠΕΙΡΑΤѠΝ

ΕΥΧΗΝ

ΟΥ ΘΕΜΙΤΟΝ ΔΕ ΠΡΟϹΑΓΕΙΝ

ΑΙΓΕΙΟΝ ΥΙΚΟΝ ΒΟΟϹ ΘΗΛΕΙΑϹ

'To Zeus, sender of fair winds, and Astarte of Palestine, and Aphrodite Urania, to the divinities that hearken, Damon son of Demetrios of Ashkelon, saved from pirates, makes this vow. It is not lawful to offer in sacrifice an animal of the goat or pig species, or a cow.' 3

The Palestinian Astarte is here distinguished from the Aphrodite of Ashkelon; and though there obviously was much confusion between them, the distinction was real. From Lucian 1 we learn that there were two goddesses, whom he keeps carefully apart, and who indeed were distinguished by their bodily form. The goddess of Hierapolis, of whose worship he gives us such a lurid description, was in human form: the goddess of Phoenicia, whom he calls Derkĕto (a Greek corruption of the Semitic Atargatis, עתר-עתי), had the tail of a fish, like a mermaid.

The name of this goddess, as written in Sidonian inscriptions, was long ago explained as a compound of עתר and עתה, ʻAtar and ʻAte. These are two well-established divine names; the former is a variant of ʻAshtart, but the latter is more obscure: it is possibly of Lydian origin. 2 In Syriac and Talmudic writings the compound name appears as Tarʻatha.

The fish-tailed goddess was already antiquated when Lucian wrote. He saw a representation of her in Phoenicia (*op. cit.* § 14), which seemed to him unwonted. No doubt he was correct in keeping the two apart; but it is also clear that they had become inextricably entangled with one another by his time. The figure of the goddess of Hierapolis was adorned with a *cestus* or girdle, an ornament peculiar to Urania (§ 32), who, as we learn from Herodotus, was regarded as the goddess of Ashkelon. There was another point of contact between the two goddesses—sacred fish were kept at their shrines. The fish-pond of Hierapolis is described by Lucian (§§ 45, 46) as being very deep, with an altar in the middle to which people swam out daily, and with many fishes in it, some of large size—one of these being decorated with a golden ornament on its fin.

To account for the mermaid shape of the Ashkelonite goddess a story was told of which the fullest version is preserved for us by Diodorus Siculus (ii. 4). 'In Syria is a city called Ashkelon, and not far from it is a great deep lake full of fishes; and beside it is a shrine of a famous goddess whom the Syrians called Derketo: and she has the face of a woman, and otherwise the entire body of a fish, for some reason such as this: the natives most skilful in legend fable that Aphrodite being offended by the aforesaid goddess inspired her with furious love for a certain youth among those sacrificing: and that Derketo, uniting with the Syrian, bore a daughter, and being ashamed at the fault, caused the youth to disappear and exposed the child in certain desert and stony places: and cast herself in shame and grief into the lake. The form of her body was changed into a fish: wherefore the Syrians even yet abstain from eating this creature, and honour fishes as gods.' The legend is told to the same effect by Pausanias (II. xxx. 3).

This legend is of great importance, for it helps us to detect the Philistine element in the Ashkelonite Atargatis. An essentially identical legend was told in Crete, the heroine being Britomartis or Dictynna. According to Callimachus' *Hymn to Artemis* Britomartis was a nymph of Gortyna beloved of Artemis, whom Minos, inflamed with love, chased over the mountains of Crete. The nymph now hid herself in the forests, now in the low-lying meadows; till at last, when for nine months she had been chased over crags, and Minos was on the point of seizing her, she leaped into the sea from the high rocks of the Dictaean mountain. But she sprang into fishers' nets (δίκτυα) which saved her; and hence the Cydonians called the nymph Dictynna, and the mountain from which she had leaped called they Dictaean; and they set up altars to her and perform sacrifices.

The myth of the Atargatis of Ashkelon fits very badly on to the Syrian deity. She was the very last being to be troubled with shame at the events recorded by Diodorus Siculus: she had no special connexion with the sea, except in so far as fishes, on account of their extreme fertility, might be taken as typical of the departments of life over which she presided. There can surely be little question that the coyness of the Cretan nymph, her leap into the sea, and her deliverance by means of something relating to fishes, has been transferred to the Ashkelonite divinity by the immigrants. The Atargatis myth is more primitive than that of Britomartis: the union from which Britomartis was fleeing has actually taken place, and the metamorphosis into a fish is of the crudest kind; the ruder Carians of the mainland might well have preserved an earlier phase of the myth which the cultured Cretans had in a measure refined.

The cult of Britomartis was evidently very ancient. Her temple was said to have been built by Daedalus. The name is alleged to mean *uirgo dulcis* 1; and as Hesychius and the *Etymologicon Magnum* give us respectively γλυκύ and ἀγαθόν as meanings of βριτύ or βρίτον, the explanation is very likely correct. The name of the barley drink, βρύτος or βρύτον, may possibly have some connexion with this word. See also the end of the quotation from Stephanus of Byzantium, *ante* p. 15.

Athenaeus (viii. 37) gives us an amusing piece of etymology on the authority of Antipater of Tarsus, to the effect that one Gatis was a queen of Syria who was so fond of fish that she allowed no one to eat fish without inviting her to the feast—in fact, that no one could eat ἄτερ Γάτιδος: and that the common people thought her name was 'Atergatis' on account of this formula, and so abstained from fish altogether. He further quotes from the *History of Asia* by Mnaseus to the effect that Atargatis was originally a tyrannous queen who forbade the use of fish to her subjects, because she herself was so extravagantly fond of this article of diet that she wanted it all for herself; and therefore a custom still prevails to offer gold or silver fish, or real fish, well cooked, which the priests of the goddess eat. Another tale is told by Xanthus and repeated by Athenaeus in the same place, that Atargatis was taken prisoner by Mopsus king of Lydia, and with her son Ἰχθύς ('fish') cast into the lake near Ashkelon (ιν τῇ περὶ Ἀσκάλωνα λίμνῃ) because of her pride, and was eaten by fishes.

Indeed, the Syrian avoidance of fish as an article of food is a commonplace of classical writers. A collection of passages on the subject will be found in Selden, *De Diis Syris*, II. iii.

Lucian further tells us (§ 4) that the temple at Sidon was said to be a temple of Astarte; but that one of the priests had informed him that it was really dedicated to Europa, sister of Cadmus. This *daughter of King Agenor* the Phoenicians honoured with a temple 'when she had vanished' (ἐπειδή τε ἀφανὴς ἐγεγόνεε), and related the legend about her that Zeus, enamoured of her, chased her, in the form of a bull, to Crete.

Here then we have distinctly a legend to the effect that a certain temple of the Syrian goddess was really dedicated to a deity who had fled from an unwelcome lover, and who was directly connected with Crete. In fact, we have here a confused version of the Britomartis legend on the Syrian coast. And when we turn to the *Metamorphoses* of Antoninus Liberalis, ch. 30, we find a version of the Britomartis story that is closely akin to the tale told by the Sidonian priest to Lucian. We read there that 'of Cassiepeia and Phoenix *son of Agenor* was born Carmē: and that Zeus uniting with the latter begat Britomartis. She, fleeing from the converse of men, wished to be a perpetual virgin. And first she came to Argos from Phoenicia, with Buzē, and Melitē, and Maera, and Anchiroē, daughters of Erasinos; and thereafter she went up to Cephallenia from Argos; and the Cephallenians call her Laphria; and they erected a temple to her as to a deity. Thereafter she went to Crete, and Minos seeing her and being enamoured of her, pursued her; but she took refuge among fishermen, and they caused her to hide in the nets, and from this the Cretans call her Dictynna, and offer sacrifices to her. And fleeing from Minos, Britomartis reached Aegina in a ship, with a fisherman Andromēdes, and he laid hands on her, being desirous to unite with her; but Britomartis, having stepped from the ship, fled to a grove where there is now her temple, and there she vanished (ἐγένετο ἀφανής); and they called her Aphaea, and in the temple of Artemis the Aeginetans called the place where Britomartis vanished Aphaē, and offered sacrifices as to a deity.' The relationship to Agenor, the love-chase, and the curious reference to 'vanishing' can scarcely be a mere coincidence. Lucian, though careless of detail and no doubt writing from memory, from the report of a priest who being a Syrian was not improbably inaccurate, has yet preserved enough of the Britomartis legend as told in Sidon to enable us to identify it under the guise of the story of Europa.

To the same Cretan-Carian family of legends probably belongs the sea-monster group of tales which centre in Joppa and its neighbourhood. The chief among them is the story of Perseus the Lycian hero and Andromeda; and a passage in Pliny seems to couple this legend with that of Derketo. [1] Some such story as this may have suggested to the author of the Book of Jonah the machinery of his sublime allegory; and no doubt underlies the mediaeval legends of St. George and the Dragon, localized in the neighbouring town of Lydd. We can scarcely avoid seeing in these tales literary parallels to the beautiful designs which the Cretan artists evolved from the curling tentacles of the octopus.

We are now, I think, in a position to detect a process of evolution in these tangled tales. We begin with a community dwelling somewhere on the sea-coast, probably at the low cultural level of the tribes who heaped the piles of midden refuse on the coasts of Eastern Denmark. These evolved, from the porpoises and other sea-monsters that came under their observation, the conception of a mermaid sea-goddess who sent them their food; and no doubt prayers and charms and magical formulae were uttered in her name to ensure that the creeks should he filled with fish. The sacredness of fish to the goddess would follow as a matter of course, and would be most naturally expressed by a prohibition against eating certain specified kinds. [1] And aetiological myths would of course be developed to account for her fish-tail shape. The Dictynna legend, with a *Volksetymologie* connecting the name of the nymph with a fishing-net, is one version; the legend afterwards attached to Atargatis is another.

When the Carian-Cretan league, after their repulse from Egypt, settled on the Palestine coast, they of course brought their legends with them. In their new home they found a *Bona Dea* all powerful, to whom *inter alia* fish were sacred, and with her they confused their own *Virgo Dulcis*, patroness of fishermen. They built her temples—a thing unheard-of before in Palestine—and told of her the same tales that in their old home they had told of Britomartis. They transferred the scene of the tragedy from the eastern headland of Crete to the λίμνη of Ashkelon, and they fashioned the legend into the form in which it ultimately reached the ears of Diodorus Siculus.

To the legend of Atargatis Diodorus adds that the exposed child was tended and fed by doves till it was a year old, when it was found by one Simma, who being childless adopted it, and named it *Semiramis*, a name derived from the word for 'dove' in the Syrian language. In after years she became the famous Babylonian queen: and the Syrians all honour doves as divine in consequence. The etymology is of the same order as Justin's derivation of 'Sidon' from 'a Phoenician word meaning "fish"': the tale was no doubt told primarily to account for the sacredness of doves to the Syrian goddess. The goddess of Ashkelon was likewise patroness of doves, and this bird frequently figures on coins of the city.

II. DAGON was evidently the head of the pantheon of the Philistines, after their settlement in Palestine. We hear of his temple at Gaza, Ashdod, and, possibly, according to one version of the story of the death of Saul, at Beth-Shan. [2] Jerome in commenting on 'Bel boweth down, Nebo stoopeth', in Isaiah xlvi. 1 (where some versions of the Greek have *Dagon* for *Nebo*), says Dagon is the idol of Ashkelon, Gaza, and the other cities of the Philistines. [3] The important temple of Gaza is mirrored for us in the graphic story of the death of Samson, as we shall see in the following section.

In the temple of Ashdod there was an image of the god—a thing probably unknown in the rude early Canaanite shrines. Josephus (*Wars*, v. 9. 4) calls it a ξόανον, which possibly preserves a true tradition that the figure was of wood. Some interesting though obscure particulars are given us regarding it in 1 Samuel v. 1–5. The Ark, captured at Aphek, was laid up two nights in the temple. The first night the image of Dagon fell on its face before the Ark, and was replaced by 'the priests of Dagon'; the only reference we have to specifically religious functionaries among the Philistines. The second night he was fallen again, and the head of the figure and the palms of its hands were broken off and lay on the threshold.

The account of the abasement of Dagon is of considerable importance with regard to the question of the form under which he was represented. The current idea is that he was of merman form, the upper half man, the lower half fish. This theory is by modern writers derived from the mediaeval Jewish commentators: Rabbi Levi, in the third century, said that Dagon was in the figure of a man: the first statement of his half-fish form, so far as extant authorities go, is made by David Ḳimḥi, who writes, They say that Dagon had the shape of a fish front his navel downwards, because he is called Dagon [דג = fish] and upwards from his navel the form of a man, as it is said "both the palms of his bands were cut off on the threshold".' Abarbanel appears to make the god even more monstrous by supposing that it was the *upper* end which was the fishy part. But the idea must have been considerably older than Ḳimḥi. As we shall see presently, it underlies one of the readings of the Greek translation: and the attempts at etymology in the *Onomastica* 1 show clearly that the idea arose out of the accident that דג means 'a fish', while the story in 1 Samuel v requires us to picture the god with hands; coupled with vague recollections of the bodily form of the Atargatis of Ashkelon.

If we examine the passage, we note, first, that he had a head and hands, so that he must have been at least partly human. Next we observe that exactly the same phrase is used in describing both falls of the idol. The first time it was unbroken, and the priests could put it in its place again. The second time it was fallen again, but the projecting parts of it were broken off. In other words, the first fall of the statue was just as bad as the second, except that it was not broken: there is no statement made that on the second occasion the image, whatever its form, snapped across in the middle. In both cases it fell *as a whole*, being smashed the second time, just as might happen to a china vase; this would imply that what was left standing and intact was not so much any part of the statue itself, as the pedestal or some other accessory.

The difficulty lies in the words which follow the account of the fracture of the statue—וְגָד רק עליו נשאר. In the English version these are rendered 'only [the stump of] Dagon was left'. The words in brackets, for which the Hebrew gives no warrant, are inserted as a makeshift to make some kind of sense of the passage. Wellhausen ingeniously suggested omission of the ו at the end of וגד, supposing that it had been inserted by dittography before the initial נ of the following word. This would make the word mean 'only his fish was left'. But this assumes the thesis to be proved.

When we turn to the Greek Version we find that it represents a much fuller text. It reads thus: …. The passage in brackets has no equivalent in the Hebrew text: it suggests that a line has been lost from the archetype of the extant Hebrew Version. 1 If with some MSS. we omit the first χειρῶν (which makes no satisfactory sense with ἴχνη), this lost line would imply that Dagon's feet were also fallen on the threshold (ἀμαφέθ = Hebrew ותפמה.) This does not accord with the 'fish-tail' hypothesis. But, on the other hand, it shows that the fishtail conception is considerably older than Kimhi, for χειρῶν must in the first instance have been inserted by a glossator obsessed with it.

And what are we to make of πλὴν ἡ ῥάχις ὑπελείφθη? 'The backbone of Dagon was left' is as meaningless as the traditional Hebrew, if not worse. But when we look back at the Hebrew we begin to wonder whether we may not here be on the track of another Philistine word—the technical term for, let us say, the pedestal or console on which the image stood; or, it may be, some symbol associated with it. Wellhausen (*Text d. Buch. Sam.* p. 59) has put forward the suggestion that ῥάχις really depends on קר 'only'. But the translators would presumably have understood this simple word—they have indeed rendered it correctly, by πλήν. We need a *second* קר to account for ῥάχις, and such, I submit, must have stood in the Hebrew text. Some word like (let us say) דקר, especially if unintelligible to a late Hebrew copyist, would certainly drop out sooner or later from the collocation וֹנגד רקד רק. It would be very natural for the original author to use such a word, for the sake of the paronomasia; and it would fully account for ῥάχις, which in this case is not the Greek word at all, but a transliteration of an unknown word in the Hebrew original. The word ἀμαφέθ, immediately before, which has given much trouble to the copyists of the Greek text (see the numerous variants in Holmes and Parsons), is an example of an even easier word in the Hebrew being transferred to the Greek untranslated.

Further we are told that the priests and those who entered the house of Dagon—an indication that the temple was open to ordinary worshippers—did not tread on the threshold of the temple in Ashdod, in consequence, it was said, of this catastrophe; but, as the Greek translators add 'overstepping they overstepped it' (ὑπερβαίνοντες). That the explanation was fitted to a much more ancient rite we need not doubt: the various rites and observances relating to *thresholds* are widespread and this prohibition is no isolated phenomenon. [1] It is not certain whether the threshold of the Ashdod temple only was thus reverently regarded, or whether the other Dagon temples had similar observances: the latter is probable, though evidently the writer of Samuel supposed that the former was the case. The possible connexion between the Ashdod prohibition and the 'leaping on (preferably over) the threshold' of Zephaniah i. 9, has already been noted.

We must, however, face the fact that Dagon cannot be considered as exclusively a Philistine deity, even though the Semitic etymologies which have been sought for his name are open to question. There are דג 'fish', as already mentioned, and דגן 'corn'. Philo Byblios favoured the second of these. The inscription of Eshmunazar, king of Sidon, is well known to refer to Joppa and Dor as ארץ דגן, which seems at first sight to mean 'the land of Dagon'. But more probably this is simply a reference to that fertile region as 'the land of corn'. However we have, through Philo, references associating Dagon with the Phoenicians. In the Sanchuniathon cosmogony reported in the fragments of Philo we have an account of his birth from Ouranos and Ge, [1] with his brethren Ἔλος and Kronos and Baetylos; he is equated to Σίτων 'corn', which is apparently personified; and by virtue of this equation he is identified with a Ζεὺς Ἀρότριος. All this is very nebulous: and not more definite is the curious note respecting the gods Taautos, Kronos, Dagon and the rest being symbolized by sacred letters. [2] If these passages mean anything at all, they imply that the people who taught the Phoenicians the use of letters (and possibly also of baetylic stones) also imparted to them the knowledge of the god Dagon. But stories which ostensibly reach us at third hand afford a rather unsafe *apparatus criticus*.

In Palestine itself there is clear evidence of the presence of Dagon before the coming of the Philistines. A certain Dagan-takala contributed two letters [3] to the Tell el-Amarna correspondence. By ill-luck they do not mention the place of which he was apparently the chieftain, nor do they tell us anything else to the point: the one letter is merely a protestation of loyalty, the other the usual petition for deliverance from the Aramaean invaders. 'Dagan' is not here preceded by the usual determinative prefix of divinity; but neither is the name so preceded in the references to the town of Beth-Dagon in the inscriptions of Sennacherib.

This name, Beth-Dagon, appears in several Palestinian villages. They are not mentioned in the Tell el-Amarna correspondence; and we might fairly infer that they were Philistine foundations but for the fact that the name appears in the list of Asiatic towns conquered by Ramessu III at Medinet Habu—a list probably copied from an earlier list of Ramessu II. There seems no possibility of escaping the conclusion that by

 Bty-Dkn which appears in this list, is meant one of the towns called Beth-Dagon. 4

Of these villages, one was in the tribe of Asher, another in Judah. The southern village described by Jerome 5 as of large size, was in his time called Caferdago, between Diospolis and Jamnia (Lydd and Yebnah). Jerome's village is probably to be identified with a ruin known as Dajun, close by the present village of Beit Dejan; the latter has preserved the old name and is built on a mound which is possibly the old site.

Moreover, the name Dagan appears in Mesopotamia: there seems no longer to be any doubt that a certain group of cuneiform signs, relating to a deity, is to be read *Da-gān*. In Babylonia it enters into the composition of proper names of about 2400 B.C.: a king dated 2145 B.C. was Idin-Dagān and he had a son Išme-Dagān: a seal-cylinder exists of a certain Dagān-abi son of Ibni-Dagān. In Assyria we find it in the name of Dagān-bīlu-uṣur, eponym of the year 879 B.C.: and the name is several times coupled with that of Anu 1 in cosmogonies and in invocations of various Assyrian kings. The name disappears after the ninth century: the late reference to Dagon in the Hebrew version of Tobit, chap. i 2, speaking of Sennacherib being killed ותועט דגון לפני להחפלל שנבנם בשעה 'at the hour when he went in to pray to his idol Dagon', is not of any special importance.

The fragments of Berossos relate how originally the people of Babylon lived like animals, without order: but a being named Oannes rose out of the Erythraean sea, with a complete fish-body, and a man's head under the fish-head, and human feet and voice. This being was a culture-hero, teaching the knowledge of the arts, writing, building, city-dwelling, agriculture, &c., to men: he rose from the sea by day, and returned to it at sunset.

Other fragments of Berossos tell us that Oannes was followed by similar beings, who appeared from time to time under certain of the antediluvian kings. There were in all seven, the second and probably the following four being called Annedotos, and the last being called Odakon (Ὠδάκων or Ὀδάκων). The last resembles 'Dagon' in outward form: but the elaborate discussion of Hrozný 3 has shown that the comparison between the two cannot stand: that the -ων of Ὠδάκων is a mere termination: that the names Oannes and Odakon (not however Annedotos, so far as has yet been discovered) have their prototypes in Sumerian, and cannot be equated to the Babylonian and Assyrian Dagan. The sole evidence for the fish-form of Dagan therefore disappears. The statements of Damascius (*de Principiis*, c. 125) about a Babylonian divine pair, Δάχος and Δαχή 1 add nothing to the problem: as Rev. P. Boylan and Mr. Alton have both pointed out to me, the D is a mistake for an A in both cases, and the beings referred to are evidently Lahmu and Lahamu.

That Dagān and the pre-Philistine Dagon of Palestine are one and the same being can scarcely be questioned. Hrozný (*op. cit.* p. 103) points out that the difference of the vowel is no difficulty, especially as the name appears once in Assyrian as an element in a proper name in the form Dagūna. But we may perhaps ask if the post-Philistine deity was identical with the pre-Philistine god, and whether there may not have been a conflation analogous to that which has taken place between Britomartis and Atargatis.

It is relevant to notice here in passing that the Philistine religion never had any attraction for the reactionary kings of the Hebrews. Only in a rather vague passage (Judges x. 6) is there any indication of the influence of Philistine worship on that of the Israelites. Elsewhere we read of altars built to the abomination of the Zidonians, of Moab, of the Ammonites, but never of the Philistines. The solitary exception is the consultation of the Ekronite oracle, which, as we have seen, was not Philistine at all. In spite of the semitization of the Philistines during the latter part of the Hebrew monarchy, their cult still remained too exotic to attract the Semitic temperament.

Now strange though it may seem, there is a possibility that the Philistines brought with them from their western home a god whose name was similar to Dagon. We have not found any trace of him in or around Crete: the decipherment of the Minoan tablets may possibly tell us something about this in the future. But the Etruscans, kinsmen of the Philistines, had a myth of a certain Tages, who appeared suddenly 2 from the earth in the guise of a boy, and who, as they related, was their instructor in the arts of soothsaying. This took place 'when an Etruscan named Tarchon was ploughing near Tarquinii'—names which immediately recall the *Tarkhu*, *Tarkon-demos*, and similar names of Asia Minor. 3 Festus (*sub voce*) describes Tages as a 'genii filius, nepos Iouis'. As the Etruscans rejected the letter D, Tages is closely comparable to a name beginning with Dag-; and indeed the *-es* termination is probably not part of the Etruscan name, but a nominative termination added by the foreign writers who have reported the story. If the Philistines brought such a deity with them in their Syrian home, they might well have identified him with the god *Dagon*, whom they found there before them.

It is difficult otherwise to explain how Dagān, whose worship seems to have been on the whole of secondary importance, should have acquired such supreme importance among the foreigners.

But after all, the Canaanite Dagon and the hypothetical Philistine Dag- may have been one— the latter having been borrowed by the 'proto-Philistines', as we may for convenience call them, at some remote period. The intercourse which led to the adoption of clay tablets as writing materials by the Cretans at the beginning of the middle Minoan period, and to the adoption of certain details of legal procedure (if there be any value in the conjectures given in this book regarding the Phaestos disk)—may well have led to the borrowing of the god of one nation by the other.

The *Etymologicon Magnum* calls Dagon—or rather Βητάγων, substituting the place Beth-Dagon for the name of the god—ὁ Κρόνος ὑπὸ Φοινίκων.

After the collapse of the Philistine power in David's time, we hear nothing more about Dagon except the vague guesses of etymologists and mythographers. The temple, and presumably the worship of the deity, under the old name, lasted down to the time of the Maccabees in Ashdod (1 Macc. x. 83, 84). But in Gaza the case was different. Here powerful Hellenic influences introduced numerous foreign deities, which, however, there is every reason to believe were grafted on to the old local gods and *numina*. Josephus tells us of a temple of Apollo; but our leading source is the life of Porphyrius, bishop of Gaza at the end of the fourth and beginning of the fifth century, written by his friend the deacon Marcus.

This valuable little work gives us a picture of the last struggle of heathenism, of which Gaza was the storm-centre. The descriptions are terse but vivid. We see Porphyrius, after his appointment to the bishopric, making his way painfully from Diospolis (Lydd) because the heathen living in the villages on the way erected barriers to prevent his passing, and annoyed him by burning substances that gave forth fetid odours. After they had arrived, a drought fell in the same year, which the heathen ascribed to the wrath of Marna their god, on account of the coming of Porphyrius. For two months no rain fell, notwithstanding their prayers to Marna ('whom they say is Zeus') in his capacity of lord of rain. There was a place of prayer outside the city, and the whole of the heathen population frequented this for intercession to the κύριος τῶν ὄμβρων. This place was no doubt a sanctuary with an ancient tradition; most probably to be identified with the Aldioma, or place of Zeus Aldemios. This, according to the *Etymologicon Magnum*, was the name of the chief god of Gaza, and a god of fertility; probably therefore identical with Marna. ₁ We hear of the same sanctuary in the Talmud: near Gaza was a place called Yerīd or 'Ithōza (הזולטע, also written זילטא and מילטא) outside the city where an idol was worshipped. ₂ In the sequel we learn that Porphyrius took from the Aldioma the stones with which he built the church erected by him on the site of the Marneion.

Near modern Gaza is a hill, crowned by the shrine of a Muslim saint called *Sheikh Muntar*. As usual, this true believer has succeeded to the honours of a pagan divinity. Muntar means 'a watch tower'; but possibly the name is a corruption of Marna or [Brito]martis.

The name *Marna* is capable of being rendered in Aramaic, Mar-na, ₃ Our Lord,' and not improbably this is its actual meaning. If so, it is probably an illustration of the widespread dislike to, or actual prohibition of, the mention of the real name of a divinity. ₄ At some time a hesitation to name the god—who can hardly be other than Dagon—had arisen: the respectful expression 'Our Lord' had by frequent use become practically the personal name of the divinity, and had assumed a Greek form Μάρνας, with a temple called the Μαρνεῖον, the chief temple of Gaza.

It is likely that Gaza at the time claimed to be a sacred city: the rigidness of the tabu against carrying a dead body into it suggests that such an act would pollute it. The Christians had serious trouble, soon after the coming of Porphyrius, on account of the case of one Barōchus, a zealous young Christian, who was set upon by heathen outside the city and beaten, as was thought, to death. His friends happening to find him lying unconscious, wished to carry him home; but only succeeded in doing so with the greatest difficulty, owing to the uproar caused by their carrying the apparent corpse into the city.

Stirred by events of this kind, Porphyrius determined to invoke the civil power to aid him in his struggle with heathendom, and sending Marcus to Constantinople obtained an order for the closing of the temples of Gaza. As usual, however, in the East, the official responsible for the carrying out of the order did so with one hand, allowing the other hand to be 'greased' to undo the work surreptitiously. In other words, Hilarios, the adjutant sent to carry out the order, and especially charged to close the Marneion and to put a stop to the consultation of the oracle, while appearing to execute the duty committed to him, secretly took bribes to permit the rites of heathen religion to be carried on as before. Porphyrius therefore went in person to Constantinople; interviewed the empress Eudoxia; obtained her favour by the prophecy of the birth of a son to her, which was fulfilled by the birth of Theodosius; and obtained her intercession with the emperor to secure the closing of the temples. So Porphyrius returned with his suite, and was received at Gaza with jubilation on the part of the Christians, and corresponding depression on that of the Pagans.

Some valuable hints are preserved to us by Marcus of the nature of the worship thus destroyed. A few excerpts from his work may be here given.

'As we entered the city, about the place called the Four Ways, there was standing a marble pillar, which they said was Aphrodite; and it was above a stone altar, and the form of the pillar was that of an undraped woman, ἐχούσης ὅλα τὰ ἄσχημα φαινόμενα, ₁ and they all of the city used to honour the pillar, especially the women, lighting lamps and burning incense. For they used to say of her that she used to answer in a dream those who wished to enter into matrimony; and telling falsehoods they used to deceive one another.' The worship of this statue evidently retained some of the most lurid details of the High Place worship. This statue was the first to be destroyed—by a miracle, Marcus says, on the exhibition of the Cross. He is probably mindful of the prostration of Dagon on the Ark being brought into his presence.

Ten days afterwards Cynēgius, the emperor's messenger, arrived with a band of soldiers, to destroy the temples, of which there were eight—of the Sun, Aphrodite, Apollo, Korē (Persephone), Hekatē, the Hērōeion, the Tychaion or temple of the Luck (τύχη) of the city, and the Marneion, or temple of the Crete-born Zeus, the most honourable of all the temples, which has already been mentioned. Besides these there were a countless number of minor deities in the houses and the villages. The destroying party first made its way to the Marneion. The priests, however, had been forewarned, and blocked the doors of the inner chamber with great stones. In the inner chamber or *adytum* they stored the sacred furniture of the temple and the images of the god, and then fled by other exits, of which it was said there were several, opening out of the adyta of the temple in various directions. Baffled therefore for the time, the destroying party made their way to the other temples, which they demolished; Porphyrius, like another Joshua, laying under an anathema any of the Christians who should take to himself any plunder from the treasuries. This work occupied ten days, and the question of the fate of the Marneion was then discussed. Some were for razing it, some for burning it, others again wished to preserve it and after purifying it, to dedicate it for Christian worship. Porphyrius therefore proclaimed a fast with prayer for Divine guidance in the difficulty. The Divine guidance came in strange wise; and though it has nothing to do with the Philistines, the story is so curious that it is well worth relating exactly as Marcus himself tells it. As the people, fasting and praying, were assembled in the church, a child of seven years, standing with his mother, suddenly cried out in the Syrian tongue, 'Burn the temple to the ground: for many hateful things have taken place in it, especially human sacrifices. And in this manner burn ye it. Bring liquid pitch and sulphur and lard, and mix them together and smear the brazen doors therewith, and lay fire to them, and so the whole temple will burn; it is impossible any other way. And leave the outer part (τὸν ἐζώτερον) with the enclosing wall (περίβολος). And after it is burnt, cleanse the place and there build a holy church. I witness to you before God, that it may not be otherwise: for it is not I who speak, but Christ that speaketh in me.' And when they all heard they wondered, and glorified God. And this portent came to the ears of the holy bishop (Porphyrius), who stretching his hands to heaven gave glory to God and said, 'Glory to Thee, Holy Father, who hast hidden from the wise and prudent, and hast revealed even these things to babes.' When the people were dismissed from the church he summoned the child and his mother to him in the bishop's house, and setting the child apart he said to the woman, 'I adjure thee by the Son of the Living God to say if it was on thy suggestion or of some other known to thee that thy son spoke as he did concerning the Marneion.' The woman said, 'I deliver myself to the dread and awful judgement-seat of Christ, if I had fore-knowledge of any of those things that my son spoke this day. But if it seem fit to thee, behold the boy, take him and examine him with threats, and if he said these things on the suggestion of any, he will confess it in fear; if he says nothing else it will be clear that he was inspired by the Holy Spirit.' So to make a long story short, the boy was brought in, and the bishop bade him speak and say who had put these words in his mouth—brandishing a whip as he spoke. The poor bewildered child kept silence, even though 'We who were around him '—Marcus speaks as an eye-witness—repeated the questions likewise with threats. At last the child opened his mouth and made exactly the same utterance as before, but this time in Greek—a language of which, as appeared on inquiry from the mother, he was ignorant. This settled the matter, and sealed the fate of the Marneion. The bishop gave three pieces of money to the mother, but the child, seeing them in her hand, said in the Syrian tongue, 'Take it not, mother, sell not thou the gift of God for money!' So the woman returned the money, saying to the bishop, 'Pray for me and my son, and recommend us to God.' And the bishop dismissed them in peace. It is a strange coincidence that the first and last events in the recorded history of Philistia have a mantic prodigy as their central incident!

The reference to human sacrifices is for our immediate purpose the most noteworthy point in this remarkable story. The sequel was equally remarkable. The method approved by the oracle was applied, and *immediately* the whole temple, which on the first occasion had resisted their assaults, was wrapped in flames. It burnt for many days, during which there was a good deal of looting of treasures; in the course of this at least one fatal accident occurred. At the same time a house-to-house search for idols, books of sorcery, and the like relics of heathenism, was effected, and anything of the kind discovered was destroyed.

When the plan of the new church came to be discussed some were for rebuilding it after the fashion of the old temple; others for making a complete break with heathen tradition by erecting a building entirely different. The latter counsel ultimately prevailed. Important for us is the *fact* of the dispute, because, *à propos* thereof Marcus has given us a few words of description which tell us something of what the building was like. It was cylindrical, with two porticoes, one inside the other; in the middle like a ciborium (the canopy above an altar) 'puffed out' (i.e. presumably domed) but stretched upwards (= stilted), and it had other things fit for idols and suited to the horrible and lawless concomitants of idolatry. 1

This clearly takes us far away from the *megaron* plan of the old Dagon temple. We have to do with a peristyle circular building, not unlike the Roman Pantheon, but with a stilted dome and surrounded by two rows of columns (see the sketch, p. 124). The 'other things' suitable for idol-worship were presumably the adyta of which we have already heard, which must have been either recesses in the wall or else underground chambers. The apparently secret exits made use of by the priests seem to favour the latter hypothesis. Not improbably they were ancient sacred caves. I picture the temple to myself as resembling the Dome of the Rock at Jerusalem, substituting the double portico for the aisle that runs round that building.

In clearing off the ashes and *débris* of the Marneion, Porphyrius came upon certain marbles, or a 'marble incrustation'—μαρμάρωσις—which the Marna-worshippers considered holy and not to be trodden upon, especially by women. We are of course reminded of the threshold of Dagon at Ashdod, but as we have no information as to the part of the temple to which the marbles belonged, we cannot say if there was any very close analogy. Porphyrius, we are told, paved the street with these sacred stones, so that not only men, but 'women, dogs, pigs, and beasts' should be compelled to tread upon them—a proceeding which we learn caused more pain to the idolaters than even the destruction of their temple. 'But yet to this day', says Marcus, 'most of them, especially the women, will not tread on the marbles.'

On coins of Gaza of the time of Hadrian a different temple is represented, with an ordinary distyle front. This type bears the inscription GAZA MARNA, with figures of a male and female divinity, presumably Marna and Tyche. The coin is evidence that the distyle temple—the old megaron type—survived in Gaza till this time, and it is not improbable that the Marneion destroyed by Porphyrius was built immediately afterwards. The resemblance to the Dome of the Rock at Jerusalem may be more than merely superficial. This structure was built on the ruins of Hadrian's temple of Jupiter, the Dodecapylon, which he erected over the sacred Rock, when he made his determined effort to paganize the Holy City. We have no description of this building, which was already in ruins in AD. 333; but its situation seems to require a round or symmetrically polygonal structure, and the name *dodecapylon* suggests a twelve-sided building. The Dome of the Rock (an octagon) may well have been built after this model; and the Pantheon, which has also been compared with the building indicated by the account of Marcus, is likewise of the time of Hadrian. The Marneion, therefore, might have been erected under the auspices of that enthusiastic builder, or at least after the model of other buildings which he had left behind

Fig. 5. Coins of Gaza and Ashkelon:—1. Coin of Gaza showing Temple of Marna. 2. Coin of Gaza bearing the figure and name of Io, and a debased Phoenician M, the symbolic initial of Marna. 1 3. Coin of Gaza bearing the figure and name of Minos. 4. Coin of Gaza bearing the initial of Marna. 5. Coin of Ashkelon, with the sacred fishpond. 6. Coin of Ashkelon, with figure of Astarte. 7. Coin of Ashkelon, with figure bearing a dove: below, a sea-monster. 8. Coin of Ashkelon, with figure of a dove.

him in Palestine. This would give a date for the break with the tradition of the old building. The sacred marbles might well have been some stones preserved from the old structure, and on that account of peculiar sanctity.

The rest of the acts of Porphyrius do not concern us, though we may note that there was a well in the courtyard of the Marneion, as we learn from the account of a miracle performed by him soon after the erection of the church.

Jerome, in his *Life of Hilarion*, [1] narrates sundry miraculous events, especially a remarkable victory in the circus by a Christian combatant, in which even the pagans were compelled to acknowledge *Marnas victus a Christo*. Epiphanius of Constantia in his *Ancoratus*, p. 109, [2] enumerating a number of persons who have been deified, speaks of Marnas the slave of Asterios of Crete as having so been honoured in Gaza. Here again the persistent Cretan tradition appears, but what the value or even the meaning of this particular form of it may be we cannot say. Mr. Alton has ingeniously suggested to me that Epiphanios saw and misunderstood a dedicatory inscription from the old sanctuary inscribed ΜΑΡΝΑι ΑCΤΕΡΙωι ΚΡΗΤΑΓΕΝΗι.

Outside Gaza there is scarcely any hint of Marna-worship. The name is used as an expletive in Lampridius's *Life of Alexander Severus*: and Waddington 3 reports an inscription from Kanata (Kerak), built into a modern wall, and reading ΑΝΝΗΛ[Ο]C ΚΑΜΑCΑΝΟΥ ΕΠΟΗCΕ ΔΙΙ ΜΑΡΝΑι Τωι ΚΥΡΙωι. But Annēlos very likely was a native of Gaza. A well-known statue found many years ago near Gaza, and now in the Imperial Ottoman Museum at Constantinople, has been supposed to represent Marna; but there is no evidence of this. The eccentric Lady Hester Stanhope found a similar statue at Ashkelon, but destroyed it.

Certain heathenized Jews of Constantia adored as deities Marthus (or Marthys) and Marthana, the daughters of a certain false prophet of the time of Trajan, by name Elzai 4: but this is hardly more than a coincidence.

In Ashkelon, also, there was a special deity in late Pagan times. This was Ἀσκληπιὸς λεοντοῦχος, once referred to by Marinus, writing in the fifth century A. D. 5 It may be that this is the deity spoken of in the Talmud, which mentions a temple of Ṣaripa (צריפא) at Ashkelon, evidently a form of Serapis. 6 But we know nothing of 'Asclepius the lion-holder' but his name. Probably the name of the town suggested a dedication to the similarly sounding Asclepius, just as it suggested the word ΑCΦΑΛΗC on the coins of the city. Asclepius does not appear, so far as I can find, on any coins of Ashkelon. Mars, Neptune, the genius of the city, and Aphrodite Urania, are the deities generally found on the coins: once or twice the latter is represented standing on lions. 1 On other coins an erection is represented which may be the λίμν or fish-pond for which the sanctuary was famous (see fig. 5, p. 112).

Footnotes

92:1 Neither will he feel any necessity to picture John the Baptist feeding on locust-pods instead of locusts, which the fellahin still eat with apparent relish.

92:2 For Babylonian omens derived from various insects see Hunger, *Babylonische Tieromina in Mitt. vorderas. Gesell.* (1909), 3.

94:1 i. 105.

94:2 Some have compared with this the outbreak of disease consequent on the capture of the Ark. But the two are entirely independent. The Scythian disease, whatever it may have been, was not bubonic plague, and the Philistine disease was not a hereditary curse. (The Scythian disease is much more like the *cess noinden* or 'childbirth pangs' with which the men of Ulster were periodically afflicted in consequence of the curse of Macha, according to the Irish legend of the *Tain Bó Cuailnge*. This is supposed to be a distorted tradition of the custom of the *couvade*, a theory which only adds difficulties to the original obscurity of the myth.)

94:3 Clermont-Ganneau, discussing this inscription (*Acad. des Inscriptions*, 1909), acutely points out that αἴγειον, ὑικόν are neuter adjectives, depending on some such word as ζῷον, so that all animals of these species are forbidden: whereas *female* animals of the cow kind alone are forbidden, so that bulls are lawful. Such limitations of the admissible sacrificial animals are well known in analogous inscriptions: p. 95 the triple prohibition in this case probably corresponds to the triple dedication, the purpose being to secure that none of the three deities in joint ownership of the altar shall be offended by a sacrifice unlawful in his or her worship.

Other inscriptions are quoted in the same article showing a considerable intercourse between the Ashkelonites and the island of Delos.

95:1 *De Dea Syria*, 14.

95:2 See a careful discussion in Baethgen, *Beitr.* 71 ff.

96:1 'Cretes Dianam religiosissime venerantur, βριθομάρτην gentiliter nominantes quod sermone nostro sonat uirginem dulcem.'—Solinus, *Polyhistor.* ch. xvi.

98:1 'Iope Phoenicum, antiquior terrarum inundatione, ut ferunt. Insidet collem praeiacente saxo, in quo uinculorum Andromedae uestigia ostendunt; colitur illic fabulosa <Der>ceto.'— *Hist. Nat.* v. xiii. 69.

99:1 Possibly some apparently irrational prohibition of a palatable species is at the base of the half-humorous stories of the greedy queen.

99:2 Assuming the trophy to have been exposed in the same town as the body—which is nowhere stated—then even if it were actually hung in the temple of 'Ashtaroth' (i.e. Atargatis-Britomartis), there was probably a temple of Dagon also in the town, to give rise to the parallel tradition.

99:3 'Nabo autem et ipsum idolum est quod interpretatur *prophetia et divinatio*, quam post Euangelii ueritatem in toto orbe conticuisse significat. Siue, iuxta LXX, *Dagon*, qui tamen in Hebraico non habetur. Et est idolum Ascalonis, Gazae, et reliquarum urbium Philisthiim.'

100:1 ... (Vatican Onomasticon, ed. Lagarde, p. 215): 'Dagon piscis tristitiae' (Jerome, Liber interpret. hebraic. nominum, ed. Lagarde, p. 62). The analysis suggested is וא-גד. It reminds one of Stephanus of Byzantium's story about Ashdod: ....

101:1 Probably two adjacent lines ended thus:

יתשו דגון

יתשו המפתן

and the homoeoteleuton caused the scribe's eye to wander.

102:1 On the whole subject see H. C. Trumbull, *The Threshold Covenant, or the Beginning of Religious Rites* (Edinburgh, 1896).

103:1 ....—Frag. Philo Byblios 13, Müller, *Fragmm.* iii, p. 567.

103:2 ....—ib. p. 569.

103:3 Winckler, 215, 216; Knudtzon, 317, 318.

103:4 See Max Müller, *Egyptian Researches*, i. 49, plate 68.

103:5 *De situ et nominibus locorum*, ed. Lagarde, p. 138.

104:1 See Jensen, *Kosmologie der Babylonier*, pp. 449–456, and Paton's article 'Dagan' in Hastings's *Encyclopaedia of Religion and Ethics*.

104:2 Ed. Neubauer, p. 20, xlvii.

104:3 *Sumerisch-babylonische Mythen von dem Gotte Ninrag* (Mitth. der vorderas. Gesell. (1903), 5).

105:1 ....

105:2 Cf. the sudden appearances of Britomartis in Aegina, Pausanias, II. xxx. 3.

105:3 See Cic. *de Divinatione*, ii. 23.

107:1 Aldemios was probably another name of Marna. The *Etymologicon Magnum* gives us ....—*Etym. Magn.* ed: Gaisford, col. 58. 20.

107:2 Neubauer, *Geog. d. Talmud*. With Yerīd compare *'Ain Yerdeh*, the name of a spring outside the important city of Gezer.

107:3 It is probably a mere coincidence that there was a river-god of the same name at Ephesus, mentioned on coins of that city of the time of Domitian (MAPNAC or EΦECIΩN MAPNAC), as well as in an inscription from an aqueduct at Ephesus, now in the British Museum. See Roscher, *Lexicon*, s.v.

107:4 The word *Mar*, 'Lord,' is used in the modern Syrian church as a title of respect for saints and bishops. A pagan name בחירמ =(ירמ בחי, raM' has given') illustrates its application to divinity.

108:1 The fish-tail has now disappeared.

111:1 ....

112:1 ....—Damascius.

113:1 Ed. Migne, xxiii. 27.

113:2 Ed. Migne, xliii. 209: ....

113:3 Inscriptions, in Le Bas, *Voyage archéologique en Grèce* . . .

113:4 Epiphanius, *Contra Haeres*. I. xix.

113:5 ....—Marinus, *Vita Procli*, ch. 19.

113:6 Hildesheimer, *Beiträge zur Geog. Palästinas*, p. 3.

114:1 See De Saulcy, *Numismatique de la Terre Sainte*.

IV. Their Place in History and Civilization

A people, or rather a group of peoples, the remnant—the degenerate remnant if you will—of a great civilization, settled on the Palestine coast. They found before them a servile aboriginal population ready to their use, who could relieve them of the necessary but unaccustomed labour of extracting life and wealth from the prolific soil. They were thus free to cultivate the commercial facilities which were already established in the land they made their own. Gaza, Ashkelon, and Ashdod had harbours which opened the way to trade by sea. The great land route from Egypt to Babylon passed right through the heart of the country from end to end—Gaza was from the beginning the principal mart for northern Arabia: in the expressive words of Principal G. A. Smith, we hear the jingling of shekels in the very name of Ashkelon. Corn and wine were produced abundantly within their favoured territory, even in years when the rest of the country suffered famine; an active slave-trade (one of the most lucrative sources of wealth) centred in Philistia, as we learn from the bitter denunciation of Amos. Small wonder then that the lords of the Philistines could offer an enormous bribe to a wretched woman to betray her husband. Small wonder that the Philistines were the carriers and controllers of the arts of civilization in Palestine.

The settlement of the Philistines in Palestine falls in that period of fog, as we may call it, when the iron culture succeeds the bronze in the Eastern Mediterranean. Recent excavations have given us a clear-cut picture of the development of civilization during the bronze age; that wonderful history which was sketched in its barest outline in the course of Chapter I. Then a cloud seems to settle down on the world, through which we can dimly perceive scenes of turmoil, and the shifting of nations. When the mist rolls away it is as though a new world is before us. We see new powers on earth, new gods in heaven: new styles of architecture, new methods of warfare: the alphabet has been invented, and above all, iron has become the metal of which the chief implements are made. Crete and the great days of Egypt belong to the past: the glorious days of classical Greece are the goal before us. The chief interest of the Philistines lies in this, that their history falls almost entirely within this period of obscurity, when the iron age of Europe was in its birth-throes. They and their kin, the Zakkala in the east and Turisha in the west, bridge the gap between the old world and the new. It is owing to them that the reminiscences of the days of Crete were handed across a couple of troubled centuries, to form the basis of new civilizations in Greece, in Italy, and in the East.

Our materials for estimating the culture of the Philistines and their place in civilization are the following. (1) The Phaestos Disk; (2) The Medinet Habu sculptures; (3) The results of excavation in Philistia; (4) Scattered Biblical references.

(1) On the Phaestos Disk are forty-five characters. Of some of these it is not very easy to determine the signification, but others have some value as indicating the nature of the civilization of those who invented its script, and its analogues.

The writing, running from right to left, is in the same direction as the Carian inscriptions, but not as the Minoan linear tablets.

The *plumed head-dress* of the sign here called M has been referred to as being the link which connects this disk with Caria on the one hand and with the Philistines on the other. A. J. Reinach (*Revue archéologique*, Sér. V, vol. xv, pp. 26, 27) publishes Sardinian statuettes showing the same form of head-dress. The Sardinians being probably a later stage in the history of one branch of the sea-peoples, it is natural that they should show an analogous equipment.

The sign *a*, a man running, shows the simple waist-band which forms the sole body-covering of the Keftian envoys.

The sign *b*, a captive with arms bound behind, has no more covering than a girdle. The symbol *z* appears to represent a handcuff or fetter. Perhaps Samson was secured with some such fastening.

The sign *c* from its small size appears to represent a child. He is clad in a tunic fitting closely to the body and reaching barely to the hips. No doubt, as often in Egypt ancient and modern, in some of the remoter parts of Palestine and among the Bedawin, young children went naked.

Fig. *d* represents a woman. She has long flowing hair, and seems to be wearing a single garment not unlike the *fustān* of the modern Palestinian peasant, the upper part of which, however, has been dropped down over the lower so as to expose the body from the girdle upwards. Hall, in a recent article in the *Journal of Hellenic Studies*, shows that the figure has Mycenaean analogies.

Fig. *e*, with the shaved head, perhaps represents a slave. A figure-of-eight (an ownership mark in tatu) is represented on the cheek. 1

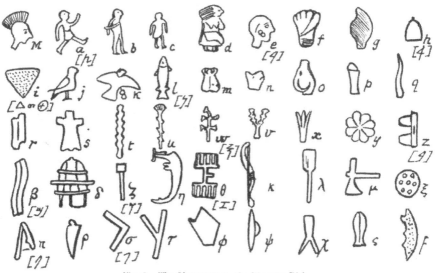

Fig. 6. The Characters on the Phaestos Disk.

Fig. *f* may represent a sandalled foot; fig. *g* may possibly represent a closed hand; but both are doubtful. Figs. *h* and *i* possibly represent a breast and *membrum muliebre* respectively, though the former may be a Phrygian cap. The interpretation of these four signs is too uncertain to allow us to attach any weight to them.

In figs. *j* and *k* we may *possibly* see the sacred doves, and in *l* the sacred fish. But this cannot be pressed. The ram's head (*o*), the hoof (*p*), the horn (*q*), and the hide (*s*) all indicate a pastoral life. The symbols *t, u, y, w, x, y* are drawn from the plant world, and it must be noticed that those who developed the script of the Disk showed an unusual appreciation of plant-shapes. It is quite remarkable to find such a variety of floral symbols.

The sign ß is probably a section of a river, suggestive of water.

The sign δ is very remarkable. It is almost certainly a representation of a domed house, such as is imitated in the Lycian tombs. It may be the prototype of one of the 'palaces of Ashdod'! The sign ζ is a pillar with a square capital. The curious sign θ may represent some kind of key.

Very important is the ship, fig. η. It is one more link with the Medinet Habu sculptures, in which, as we shall see, an identical ship makes its appearance.

The bow and arrow, figs. κ, λ, are especially interesting. Reinach (*op. cit.* p. 35) ingeniously points out that it is a true picture of the bow of the Lycian Pandarus, made of two horns of the wild goat fixed and bound on a piece of wood.

...

Iliad, iv. 105–11.

The curved poignard (ρ) has also Lycian and Carian analogies (Reinach, *op. cit.* p. 35). The axe (μ), square (σ), plane (τ), signet-ring (ψ), and leather-cutter's knife (φ), the latter perforated with a hole in the butt for suspension, all show the specializing of tools which is a characteristic of civilization.

Of especial importance is the round shield with bosses (ξ). It is not Cretan: the Cretan shield is a long oval. But the Sherdanian warriors at Medinet Habu bear the round bossed shield, and Reinach (*op. cit.* p. 30) figures an Etruscan statuette which bears an identical protection.

The other signs (π, σ, τ, χ and ϝ) are not sufficiently clear to identify (τ may be an astragalus, used in games, and π may be an adze). But enough will have been said to show that quite apart from its literary value, the Phaestos Disk is of very considerable importance as a document in the history of Aegean civilization.

(2) We now turn to the sculptures on the temple of Medinet Habu. Here we have precious illustrations of costumes, vehicles, and arms.

Fig. 7. Wagons of the Pulasati.

Fig. 8. The Head-dress of the Pulasati.

The Pulasati wear a plumed head-dress, the plumes being fitted into an elaborately embroidered band encircling the temples, and secured by a chin-strap passing in front of the ears. The other tribes wear similar head-dresses, except the Shekelesh, who have a cap. The Zakkala are represented as beardless. Their sole body-costume is the waistband, though some of them seem to have bracelets or armlets, and bands or straps crossing the upper part of the body. The women have the close-fitting *fustān;* the children are naked.

The land contingent travel in wagons, of a square box-like shape, some with framed, some with wickerwork sides. They have two solid wheels, secured to the axle by a linch-pin; and are drawn

Fig. 9. The Sea-fight between Ramessu III and the Allies.

by four oxen abreast. The sea-contingent travel in ships which show a marked resemblance to that of the Phaestos Disk. The keel is curved (more so at Medinet Habu than at Phaestos) and both bow and stem rise high above the deck, with ornamental finials. A rudder-oar projects from the stem; and at Medinet Habu (not at Phaestos) a mast rises from the middle of the boat, with a yard and a lug-sail. The ships are fitted with oars, which in the summary Phaestos hieroglyphic are not shown.

The warriors in the coalition are armed with a sword and with the long Carian spear; they have also daggers and javelins for throwing, and carry circular shields.

A number of enamelled tablets, once forming part of the decoration of the temple, have been described, 1 and these add some further valuable details. They show prisoners in full costume, not the summary fighting costume. A number of these do not concern us, being Semitic or North African; but a *Shekelesh*, a *Philistine*, and one of the *Turisha* are represented, if Daressy's identifications are to be accepted. Unfortunately there is no explanatory inscription with the figures.

The *Shekelesh* has a yellow-coloured skin, a small pointed beard, not meeting the lower lip. His hair is combed backward, in a way remarkably similar to the hair of the woman in the Phaestos disk (or he wears a crimped head-dress). He is apparelled in a gown, black with yellow circles above, green below, with vertical folds; over this is a waistband divided into coloured squares by bands of green. On his breast he wears an amulet, in the shape of a ring suspended round his neck by a cord. A sort of torque [or a chain] surrounds his neck, and his hands are secured in a handcuff.

The *Philistine* is more fully bearded: he has likewise a yellow-coloured skin. The top of the tablet is unfortunately broken, so only the suggestion of the plumed head-dress is to be seen. He wears a long white robe with short sleeves, quatrefoil ornament embroidered upon it, and with some lines surrounding the neck; over this is a waistband extending from the knees up to the breast, with elaborate embroidery upon it: a tassel hangs in the middle. On the arms are bracelets. The face of this prisoner is of a much more refined cast than any of the others.

The supposed *Turisha* has a red skin: his costume resembles that of the Philistine, but it is less elaborately embroidered. Three long ornamental tassels hang from the waistband.

(3) In a country like Palestine, frequently plundered and possessing a climate that does not permit of the preservation of frescoes and similar ancient records, we cannot hope to find anything like the rich documentation that Egypt offers us on the subject of commerce. Some suggestive facts may, however, be learnt from finds made in recent excavations, more especially pottery with coloured decoration. This will be found described in the section on pottery in my *Excavation of Gezer*, vol. ii, pp. 128–241.

Fig. 10. A Bird, as painted on an Amorite and a Philistine Vase respectively.

Putting aside details, for which I may refer the reader to that work, it may be said that the periods, into which the history down to the fall of the Hebrew monarchy is divided, are five in number; to these have been given the names pre-Semitic, and First to Fourth Semitic. The Second Semitic, which I have dated 1800–1400 B.C., the time which ends in the Tell el-Amarna period, shows Egyptian and Cypriote influence in its pottery, and here for the first time painted ornament becomes prominent. The figures are outlined in broad brush strokes, and the spaces are filled in afterwards, wholly or partly, with strokes in another colour. The subjects are animals, birds, fishes, and geometrical patterns generally, and there can be little doubt that they are crude local imitations of models of Late Minoan ware, directly imported into the country. The Third Semitic, 1400–1000 B.C., includes the time of the Philistine supremacy: and though I have dated the beginning of the period rather earlier than the time of their arrival, the peculiar technique of painted pottery that distinguishes it need not be dated so early, and may well have been introduced by them, as it certainly comes to an abrupt end about the time of their fall. In this there is a degeneration observable as compared with the best work of the Second Semitic ware. The designs had in fact become 'hieratic', and the fine broad lines in several colours had given place to thin-line monochrome patterns, which will be found illustrated in the book referred to.

The Philistines thus, in this particular art, show an inferiority to their Semitic predecessors. The reason is simple: they were removed farther in time from the parent designs. But the sudden substitution of the fine-line technique of the Third Semitic period for the broad-line technique of the Second, while the general plan of the designs remains the same, can be most easily accounted for by the assumption that the art passed from one race to another. And the sudden disappearance of the fine-line technique coincides so completely with the subjugation of the Philistines, that we can hardly hesitate to call painted ware displaying the peculiar Third Semitic characters 'Philistine'. This may be a valuable help for future exploration.

The five graves found at Gezer, of which a fully illustrated detailed description will be found in *Excavation of Gezer*, vol. i, pp. 289–300, were so absolutely different from native Palestinian graves of any period that unless they were those of Philistines or some other foreign tribe they would be inexplicable. They were oblong rectangular receptacles sunk in the ground and covered with large slabs. Each contained a single body stretched out (not crouched, as in the Canaanite interments), the head, with one exception, turned to the east. Ornaments and food-deposits were placed around. The mouth-plate found on some of the skeletons was an important link with Cretan tradition, and the graves, as a whole, show decided kinship with the shaft-graves of Knossos or Mycenae, although naturally the art-centre has shifted to Cyprus, which was the origin of such of the deposits as had no Egyptian analogies. The bones from these tombs presented analogies with Cretan bones (see p. 60 *ante*); but of course five skeletons are quite insufficient as a basis for anthropological deductions.

With further excavation the debt of Palestinian civilization to the Philistines will probably be found to be even greater than the foregoing paragraphs would suggest. Briefly, the impression which the daily study of objects found in excavation has made on the present writer is, that from about 1400–1200 B.C. onwards to about 800 B.C. Western Palestine was the scene of a struggle between the Aegean and Egyptian civilizations, with a slight mingling of Mesopotamian influence, and that the local tribes took a merely passive interest in the conflict and made no contribution whatever to its development.

(4) The Biblical and other literary sources point to the same conclusion.

Let us take as an illustration the art of Architecture. It is notable that the only Palestine temples we read about in the Old Testament, until the building of Solomon's temple, are the houses of the Philistine deities. [1] Yahweh has a simple tent; the Canaanite deities have to be content with their primitive High Places—open areas of ground with rude pillar-stones. But

Gaza, Ashdod, and Beth-Shan have their temples, and most likely the place called Beth-Car and some of the Beth-Dagons derived their Semitic names from some conspicuous temples of gods of the Philistine pantheon.

We can deduce something as to the architecture of the Gaza temple from the account of its destruction by Samson (Judges xvi). There were two groups of spectators—a large crowd (the figure 3000 need not be taken literally) on the roof, and the lords and their attendants inside. If Samson was also inside, those on the roof could not have seen him, for no *hypaethrum* of any probable size would have allowed any considerable number to enjoy the sport. Samson must therefore have been outside the temple; and it follows that the lords and their attendants must have been, not in an enclosed *naos*, but under an open portico. That is to say, the structure must have been a building of the *megaron* type. When Samson rested—just where we should expect, at the edge of the grateful shade of the portico, where he could the more quickly recover his strength but would be at a respectful distance from the Philistine notables—he seized the wooden pillars of the portico, which probably tapered downwards in the Mycenean style. He pushed them off their bases by 'bowing himself with all his might', and, the portico being distyle and having thus no other support, he brought the whole structure down. Only a *megaron* plan will satisfy all the conditions of the story.

Buildings such as this must have been familiar to David in Gath, and perhaps the sight of them suggested to his mind the idea of erecting a more worthy temple to his own Deity, as soon as he came into his kingdom. And when the work was carried out by Solomon, we see that the same model was followed.

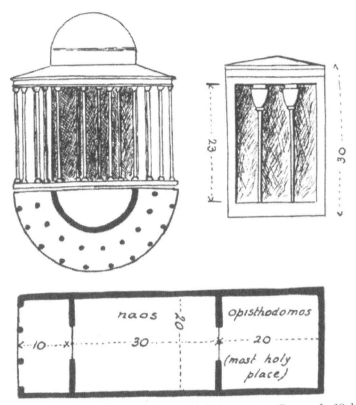

Fig. 11. Sketch-plans and Elevations of the Marneion at Gaza and of Solomon's Temple (accessory buildings omitted). The dimensions of the latter are figured in cubits: the former is not to scale.

The description in 1 Kings vi, vii is not an architect's specification, and it has numerous technical terms hard to understand. Many attempts have been made to design a building which should conform to this account, helped out by the not always trustworthy Josephus. The mutual incompatibility of these restorations (to say nothing of their *prima facie* architectural improbability) is sufficient to deter the present writer from attempting to add to their number. The main lines of the description are, however, clear enough to show with what kind of building we have to deal. We need not attempt to assign a place to the subsidiary external buildings in three stories, their winding stairs and other appurtenances, erected against the outside of the main structure. But we note that the latter was oblong, 60 cubits long, 30 cubits high, and 20 cubits broad. These figures show a classical sense of *proportion* for which we look in vain in any ancient building that excavation has revealed in Palestine. A portico in front, of the breadth of the house, was 20 cubits broad and 10 cubits deep. Here again the dimensions are proportioned. The portico was distyle, like that in the temple of Gaza: the two pillars were called by names which show that they were NOT massēbōth—'the stablisher' and 'strength in it' are very suitable names for pillars that have to bear the responsibility of keeping up a heavy portico. These pillars had shafts 18 cubits long, and capitals 5 cubits high—a total length of 23 cubits, which leaves, when subtracted from the height of the building, 7 cubits, a margin that is just about sufficient for the entablature above and the plinth below. At the opposite end of the building 'the oracle' or 'the most holy place' corresponds exactly to the *opisthodomos*. It was 20 cubits square, which left a *naos*, measuring 30 cubits by 20, in the middle of the building: the 'forty cubits' of 1 Kings vi. 16 evidently includes the portico.

With regard to the ordinary domestic architecture of the Philistines, it must be admitted that the excavations which have been made in Philistine towns do not lead us to infer that they were on the whole much better housed than their Semitic neighbours. Amos, is true, speaks of the 'palaces' of Gaza and Ashdod (i. 8, iii. 9); but this is rather a favourite word (מנמרות) of the prophet's, and he finds 'palaces' in other towns as well. To a rough herdsman many buildings would look palatial, which when viewed from another standpoint would hardly make the same impression.

One of the Philistine tombs at Gezer contained a small knife of iron; and this leads us at once to a discussion of fundamental importance.

Inserted into the account of the battle of Michmash there is a very remarkable passage (1 Sam. xiii. 19–23). It is corrupt, and some parts of it cannot be translated, but the meaning of it seems to be something like this: 'Now there was no smith found throughout all the land of Israel, for the Philistines said, "Lest the Hebrews make them sword or spear." But all the Israelites went down to the Philistines to sharpen every man his share, and his coulter, and his axe and his ox-goad (?).' The next verse is too corrupt to translate, and then the passage proceeds: 'In the day of battle there was neither sword nor spear in the hand of any of the people, except with Saul and Jonathan themselves.'

This is sometimes referred to as a 'disarmament', but there is no hint of anything of the kind. It simply says that the Philistines kept the monopoly of the iron trade in their own hands, and naturally restricted the sale of weapons of offence to the Hebrews, just as modern civilized nations have regulations against importing firearms among subject or backward communities. The Hebrews were just emerging from the bronze age culture. Iron agricultural implements, which seem slightly to precede iron war-weapons, had been introduced among them 1; but the novelty of iron had not worn off by the time of Solomon when he built his temple without the profaning touch of this metal (1 Kings vi. 7)—just as when Joshua made flint knives to perform the sacred rite of circumcision (Joshua v. 2); the old traditions must be maintained in religious functions. The champions of the Philistines, of course, were able to use iron freely, although for defensive purposes they still use bronze. 2

Goliath had a bronze helmet, a bronze cuirass of scale-armour (not a mail-coat, as in the English translation), bronze greaves, and a bronze 'javelin', but a spear with a great shaft and a heavy head of iron. The armour of 'Ishbi-benob' was probably similar, but the text is corrupt and defective. The armour of Goliath is indeed quite Homeric, and very un-Semitic. The κυνέν πάγχαλκος, the χαλκοκνήμιδες, 3 and the enormous spear—

... 4—

are noteworthy in this connexion, especially the greaves, the Hebrew word for which (מצחת) occurs nowhere else. The θώραξ λεπιδωτός alone would seem post-Homeric, but this is an *argumentum e silentio*. Fragments of a scale-cuirass, in iron, and of a rather later date, were found in the excavation of Tell Zakariya, overlooking the scene where the battle is laid (*Excavations in Palestine*, p. 150). But the culture that Goliath's equipment illustrates, like his ordeal by single combat, is much more European or Aegean than Palestinian.

In the report of Wen-Amon we found that the Zakkala were busy in the Phoenician ports, and had large influence in Phoenicia. The representations of Phoenician ships, such as the sadly damaged fresco which W. Max Müller has published, 1 shows them to have been identical in type with the ships of the Pulasati. It is highly probable that further research will show that it was due to the influence of the 'Peoples of the Sea' that the Phoenicians were induced to take to their very un-Semitic seafaring life. And it is also probable that it was due to Zakkala influence that the same people abandoned the practice of circumcision, as Herodotus says they did when they had commerce with 'Greeks'. 2

An interesting question now arises. Was it to the Philistines and their kinsmen that the civilized world owes the alphabet? The facts that suggest this query may be briefly stated. For countless generations the Egyptians, the Babylonians, and probably the Hittites, had been lumbering away with their complex syllabaries; scripts as difficult to learn and to use as is the Chinese of to-day. As in China, the complexity of the scripts was a bar to the diffusion of learning: the arts of reading and writing were perforce in the hand of specially trained guilds of scribes. No one thought of the possibility of simplifying the complexities; while current 'hieratic' forms of the letters might come into being with hasty writing, all the elaborate machinery of syllables and ideograms and determinatives was retained without essential modification.

Suddenly we find that a little nation in Syria appears to have hit upon a series of twenty-two easily-written signs by which the whole complex system of the sounds of their language can be expressed with sufficient clearness. If it was really the Phoenicians, of all people, who performed this feat of analysis, it was one of the most stupendous miracles in the history of the world. That the Phoenicians ever originated the alphabet, or anything else, becomes more and more impossible to believe with every advance of knowledge.

The alphabet makes its appearance soon after the movements of the 'sea-peoples'. Zakar-Baal is found keeping his accounts, not on clay tablets (and therefore not in cuneiform) but on papyrus, which he imports from Egypt in large quantities. And we are tempted to ask if the characters he used were some early form of the signs of the so-called 'Phoenician' alphabet.

The oldest specimen of this alphabet yet found has come to light in Cyprus: the next oldest is the far-famed Moabite Stone. W. Max Müller 1 cleverly infers from some peculiarities in the rendering of names in the list of Sheshonk's captured towns, that the scribe of that document was working from a catalogue in which the names were written in the Phoenician alphabet. This would bring the use of this alphabet in Palestine back to about 930 B.C., or about a century earlier than the Moabite Stone. A letter in neo-Babylonian cuneiform, probably not much earlier than this, and certainly of local origin, was found at Gezer: the date of the introduction of the Phoenician alphabet is thus narrowed down very closely.

Whence came the signs of this alphabet? De Rougé's theory, which derived them from Egyptian hieratic, was the most reasonable of any, but no longer commands favour. There was for long a script of linear signs, strangely resembling the Phoenician alphabet, in use in Crete. It must be admitted, however, that so far no very satisfactory analogies have been drawn between them, though their comparison is not without promise of future fruit.

But in this connexion the Phaestos Disk once more seems to assume importance. We are inclined to ask if it is possible that in the script of which this document is so far the sole representative, we are to see the long-sought origin? It is not unreasonable to suppose that in process of time the script of the Disk would become simplified into just such a linear script as that alphabet: and the principle of elision of the terminal vowel of syllables, already noticed in analysing the inscription on the Disk, is just what is wanted to help the process of evolution over that last most difficult fence, which divides a syllabary from a pure alphabet. Suppose that three syllables, *ka, ko, ku*, represented each by a special symbol, lost their vowel under certain grammatical or euphonic conditions; then all three being simply pronounced *k* might in writing become confused, leading ultimately to the choice of one of the syllabic signs to denote the letter *k*. Thus an alphabet of consonants would develop, which is just what we have in the Phoenician alphabet. The 45 +*x* characters of the original script—for we have no guarantee that we have all the characters of the script represented on the disk—could very easily wear down by some such process as this to the twenty-two signs of the Phoenician alphabet.

As to the forms of the letters, in the total absence of intermediate links, and our total ignorance of the phonetic value of the Phaestos signs, it would be premature to institute any elaborate comparisons between the two scripts. The Phaestos Disk is dated not later than 1600 B.C., the Phoenician alphabet cannot be traced even so far back as about 1000 B.C., and what may have happened in the intervening six hundred years we do not know. But some arresting comparisons are already possible. The symbol which I have called (h) might well in rapid writing develop into the Phoenician sign *aleph*. The little man running (a) is not unlike some forms of *tzade*. The head (e) both in name and shape reminds us of *rēsh*. The dotted triangle (i) recalls *daleth* or *teth*, the fish (l) in name and to some extent in shape suggests *nun*—it is notable that the fish on the Disk always stands upright on its tail—the five-leaved sprig (w) is something like *samekh*, the water-sign (ß) might be *mem* (the three teeth of the Phoenician letter preserving the three lines of the original sign). The manacles (z) resembles *beth*, the nail-pillar or prop (ζ) resembles nay in both shape and meaning, the remarkable key (θ) simplifies into *zayin*, the square (σ) into *gimel*, and the object (π) whatever it may be, into *pe*. These tentative equivalents have been added for comparison to the table of characters on p. 116. The direction of writing is from right to left in each case.

The plumed head-dress, so conspicuous as a sign on the Disk, connects it with the Philistines: and the evidence of forded us by the Golénischeff papyrus of the Syrian colonies of Philistines, or of their near kinsmen the Zakkala, links it with the Phoenicians. How far it may be possible to make further comparisons, with the various scripts of Crete, Cyprus, and Asia Minor, are questions which must be left for future discoveries and for special research.

We are not here writing a history of the alphabet: but one or two points may be noticed which have a bearing on the subject. It is commonly assumed that because the names of the letters have a meaning in Semitic, and no meaning in Greek, therefore they are Semitic words adapted into Greek. This is, however, a *non sequitur*. [1] It would be more probable that the *borrowing* nation should cast about for words similar in sound, and possessing a meaning which would make the names of the letters easily remembered. Such an attempt would be sure to be unsuccessful in some cases: and in point of fact there are several letter-names in the Semitic alphabet to which the tortures of the Inquisition have to be applied before a meaning can be extracted from them through Semitic. It may thus be that all the letter-names are a heritage from some pre-Hellenic, non-Semitic language: and instead of the old idea of a Phoenician *Ur-Alphabet* from which all the South Semitic, North African, West Asian, Hellenic, and Italic alphabetic scripts are derived, we are to picture a number of parallel and nearly related alphabets developing out of one of the hieroglyphic syllabaries of the Aegean basin—one of which scripts was taught to the Phoenicians by the despised Philistines. Whoever invented the alphabet laid the foundation-stone of civilization. Can it be that we owe this gift to the Philistines, of all people?

And even this is not all. The rude tribes of Israel were forced to wage a long and stubborn fight with the Philistines for the possession of the Promised Land. For long it seemed doubtful whether Canaan would be retained by the Semitic tribes or lost to them: and it is no mere accident that the best-known name of the country is derived from that of the sea-rovers. In the struggle the Hebrews learned the lessons of culture which they needed for their own advancement: and what was more important, they learned their own essential unity. The pressure of external opposition welded, as nothing else could have done, their loosely-knitted clans into a nation. This was the historic function of the Philistines; they accomplished their task, and then vanished with startling suddenness from the stage. But the Chosen People were led on from strength to strength, till they too fulfilled their mission of teaching mankind to look forward to a time when the knowledge of the Lord should cover the earth as the waters cover the sea.

Thus the influence of the Philistines remains, even if indirectly, a heritage of humanity to the end of time.

Footnotes

116:1 Compare the scarified lines still to be seen on the faces of negroes who have been liberated from slavery within recent years in the Turkish empire.

120:1 Daressy, 'Plaquettes émaillées de Médinet Habu,' in *Annales du Service des Antiquités de l'Égypte*, vol. xi, p. 49.

123:1 Except the temple at Shechem (Judges viii. 33–ix. 46). The events described as taking place there certainly postulate a covered building. This, however, is perhaps no real exception: it may have originally been a Philistine structure. It was dedicated to a certain *Baal-* or *El-Berith*. But 'the Lord of the Covenant' is a strange name for a local *ba'al*: can it be that *Berith* is a corruption of Βριτο[μαρτις]? The Book of Judges was probably written about the sixth century B.C.: by then the temple was most likely a ruin, and the memory of its dedication might easily have become obscured. The curious expression in Ezekiel, commented upon on p. 6 *ante*, might be similarly explained: by the ordinary canons of criticism the difficult original reading is to be preferred to the easy emendation there quoted.

126:1 See the essay on 'Bronze and Iron' in Andrew Lang's *The World of Homer*, pp. 96–104.

126:2 An elaborate paper, entitled 'Die Erfinder der Eisentechnik', by W. Belck, will be found in *Zeitschrift für Ethnologie* (1907), p. 334. It claims the Philistines as the original inventors of the smith's art. That is, perhaps, going a little too far.

126:3 Greaves appear to be unknown in Oriental or Egyptian warfare. See Daremberg and Saglio, *Dict. des antt. gr. et rom.*, s. v. *Ocrea*.

126:4 Il. vi. 318.

127:1 *Mitth. der vorderas. Gesell.* (1904), 2, plate iii.

127:2 Il. 104.

128:1 *Asien and Europa*, p. 171.

129:1 See M. René Dussaud's paper 'L'Origine égéenne des alphabets sémitiques' in *Journal asiatique*, Sér. X, vol. v, p. 357.

Made in the USA
Lexington, KY
04 June 2016